GuitaRevolution

Lessons from
the Groundbreakers
& Innovators

By Jesse Gress

Backbeat
Books

San Francisco

Published by Backbeat Books
600 Harrison Street, San Francisco, CA 94107
www.backbeatbooks.com
email: books@musicplayer.com

An imprint of the Music Player Network
Publishers of *Guitar Player, Bass Player, Keyboard, EQ,* and other magazines
United Entertainment Media. Inc.
A CMP Information company

CMP
United Business Media

Copyright © 2005 by Jesse Gress. All rights reserved. No part of this book covered by copyrights hereon may be reproduced or copied in any manner whatsoever without written permission, except in the case of brief quotations embodied in articles and reviews. For information, contact the publishers.

Distributed to the book trade in the US and Canada by
Publishers Group West, 1700 Fourth Street, Berkeley, CA 94710

Distributed to the music trade in the US and Canada by
Hal Leonard Publishing, P.O. Box 13819, Milwaukee, WI 53213

Text design and composition by Chris Ledgerwood
Cover design by Richard Leeds — BigWigDesign.com
Front cover photo by Jay Blakesberg

ISBN-13: 978-0-87930-868-1
ISBN-10: 0-87930-868-0

Printed in the United States of America

05 06 07 08 09   5 4 3 2 1

Contents

Introduction

Welcome to the (r)evolution. The extraordinary artists profiled in these pages share a bond that extends far beyond their choice of musical instrument. These guitarists—a diverse group of technically accomplished and emotionally moving players capable of eliciting a high WTFF (see Vernon Reid lesson)—belong to that special breed that has managed to alter our perception of the instrument. They *fomented* things.

The commitment of these players is undeniable and unquestionable. No part-timers here—these folks have eaten, breathed, and slept guitar for most of their adult lives. There's simply no other way to become *that* good. Through tireless devotion, happy accidents, divine inspiration, and who knows what else, each of these individualists ignored popular musical trends, followed his inner muse, and left an indelible mark on the way guitarists approach their instrument. And, in doing so, they have heroically opened the public ear to new sounds and made it safer for us to stretch our own musical wings. We owe them, big time.

Culled from lessons I wrote for *Guitar Player* during my tenure as music editor, these chapters fall into three categories: Private Lesson, created with the direct participation of the artist; Style Lesson, a thesis-level stylistic analysis; and Solo Transcription, a note-by-note rendering of a solo or complete song. For nine years of publication, I had the good fortune to immerse myself in the music of the masters on a monthly basis, and it's thrilling to see the cream of the crop represented in a single edition. (If certain names are conspicuous in their absence—Clapton, Page, Richards, Van Halen, and Blackmore come to mind—it's because their lessons have been republished in other recent Backbeat titles, such as the *How To Play* series.)

GuitaRevolution provides a glimpse into the musical minds of 16 of the most innovative visionaries in the annals of guitar lore. From Les Paul (arguably the first rock guitarist), Jeff Beck, and Jimi Hendrix to Steve Vai, Stevie Ray Vaughan, and Michael Hedges, each has had a profound and lasting effect on the evolution of our beloved instrument and the select group that plays it. Those who are still with us continue to push the envelope, while those who are not live on through a rich legacy of invaluable recordings.

Speaking of recordings, while you're learning licks like the ones in *GuitaRevolution*, there's no substitute for actually hearing the music. That's why we've teamed with TrueFire.com to give you free online audio for most of the examples in the book. Check page viii.

The sheer amount of collective musical experience represented in these pages is astonishing. Take your time, digest these morsels of wisdom slowly and deliberately, and savor every bite. Who knows? You may be inspired to carry the torch into uncharted territories and join the ranks of the groundbreakers and innovators as the GuitaRevolution marches on.

— Jesse Gress

Notational Symbols

The following symbols are used in *GuitaRevolution* to notate fingerings, techniques, and effects commonly used in guitar music. Certain symbols are found in either the tablature or the standard notation only, not both. For clarity, consult both systems.

4● : Left-hand fingering is designated by small Arabic numerals near note heads (1=first finger, 2=middle finger, 3=third finger, 4=little finger, t=thumb).

p● : Right-hand fingering designated by letters (p=thumb, i=first finger, m=middle finger, a=third finger, c=little finger).

②● : A circled number (1-6) indicates the string on which a note is to be played.

⊓ : Pick downstroke.

V : Pick upstroke.

Bend: Play the first note and bend to the pitch of the equivalent fret position shown in parentheses.

Reverse Bend: Pre-bend the note to the specified pitch/fret position shown in parentheses. Play, then release to indicated pitch/fret.

Hammer-on: From lower to higher note(s). Individual notes may also be hammered.

Pull-off: From higher to lower note(s).

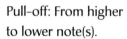

Slide: Play first note and slide up or down to the next pitch. If the notes are tied, pick only the first. If no tie is present, pick both.

A slide symbol before or after a single note indicates a slide to or from an undetermined pitch.

Finger vibrato.

Bar vibrato.

Bar dips, dives, and bends: Numerals and fractions indicate distance of bar bends in half-steps.

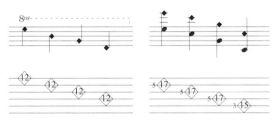

Natural harmonics.   Artificial harmonics.

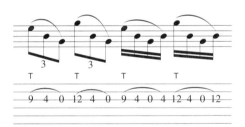

Pick-hand tapping: Notes are hammered with a pick-hand finger, usually followed by additional hammer-ons and pull-offs.

Trill.

Tremolo picking.   Strum: Arrow heads indicate direction.

HOW TABLATURE WORKS

The horizontal lines represent the guitar's strings, the top line standing for the high *E*. The numbers designate the frets to be played. For instance, a 2 positioned on the first line would mean play the 2nd fret on the first string (0 indicates an open string). Time values are indicated on the standard notation staff seen directly above the tablature. Special symbols and instructions appear between the standard and tablature staves.

CHORD DIAGRAMS

In all chord diagrams, vertical lines represent the strings, and horizontal lines represent the frets. The following symbols are used:

—— Nut; indicates first position.

X Muted string, or string not played.

○ Open string.

⌒ Barre (partial or full).

● Placement of left-hand fingers.

III Roman numerals indicate the fret at which a chord is located.

Arabic numerals indicate left-hand fingering.

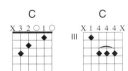

GUITAREVOLUTION

FREE AUDIO LESSONS

All of the lessons featured in GUITAREVOLUTION are available online, in audio MP3 format, for immediate download AT NO EXTRA COST. Now you can hear how the lesson examples are supposed to sound when played by the pros. Get your free audio lessons now and start learning the basics and beyond!

How to Get Your Earful

1) Go to www.GuitaRev.TrueFire.com.
2) Register the Backbeat code printed on the inside back cover of this book.
3) Download lessons to your desktop.

$10 Bonus From TrueFire!

If you're new to TrueFire, after registering and downloading your lessons, you will be e-mailed a TrueFire Cash certificate good for $10 worth of additional lessons on TrueFire. Choose from over 1,200 killer guitar lessons written and performed by top artists and instructors.

TrueFire.com
ignited we stand™

Les Paul

"Caravan"

Originally published in Guitar Player, *December 1998.*

Released in 1948, "Caravan" is one of the earliest examples of Les Paul's studio wizardry. At the time, multitrack tape recorders didn't exist. To record the song's layered guitars, Paul had to cut a part on a disc, then, accompanied by that record, capture the combined live and recorded performances onto a second disc. He'd repeat the process until he had an orchestra of "multitracked" guitars.

"Once I got the hang of it, the music just exploded," Paul recalls. "I had so many ideas. I recorded 'Caravan' and then went right to the next song. Picture this: Between 1945 and 1948, I recorded 'Lover,' 'Caravan,' 'What Is This Thing Called Love?'—a whole bunch of songs. I took 'Lover' up to Capitol Records, and they flipped over it. I hadn't put the solos on the rest of the songs. I told Capitol, 'Every day that goes by, I'm gonna get better. When you're ready for the next record, I'll put a solo on it. By then I'll have better ideas.'

"Right after that I had an automobile accident. I came out with my arm in a cast, and here I am with all these crazy ideas and no solos! The only thing that moved was my thumb, so using a thumb-pick, I played the melody for 'Caravan' on a headless aluminum guitar I'd built in 1942, laid flat on a stand. Prior to the accident, everything I'd recorded—including the half-speed stuff—I'd played on my clunker, an old Epiphone [the infamous "log" guitar] that I'd rebuilt in 1941. That was the baby that really raised all the hell and was probably one of the biggest influences on Fender, Gibson—everybody."

Though Paul commonly recorded his guitar direct, he played "Caravan" and "Lover" through a Fender combo. "I used a model Leo built before he came out with the Twin Reverb," he reveals.

Dissecting Paul's music is an illuminating yet startling experience. Paul would record some of his guitar overdubs at half-speed. When played back at normal speed, these lines would double their tempo and jump up an octave.

Play the recording of "Caravan" at half-speed and you'll hear the song's pixie guitars at their original pitch and tempo. But beware! The guitars Paul recorded at normal speed now sound an octave lower. In this sonic space, the woozy combination of slowed-down and normal guitars is surreal enough to induce a dreamlike trance. "Exactly!" Paul laughs. "More like a nightmare."

Not all of Paul's sped-up guitars were recorded at half-speed. "I had different-diameter pulleys to run the discs at different speeds," he elaborates, "but 'Caravan' was half-speed."

"Caravan" was originally recorded in the key of F minor, though it's in F# minor on Capitol's Les Paul box set (*The Legend and the Legacy*). When I tell Paul this, he seems genuinely surprised: "It's up a half-step? That wasn't intentional. It must have been sped up somewhere along the way."

Our score (**Ex. 1**) comprises the four-bar intro and the first 16 bars of the melody arranged for four guitars and pump organ. Some performance notes:

- Guitar 1 is the thumb-picked melody.
- The pump organ is arranged for guitar in the score.
- Guitar 2, notated as it sounds on the final recording, plays the tinkerbell fills that Les recorded one octave lower at half-speed.
- Guitar 3 covers the bass.
- Guitar 4 taps—yes, *taps*—repetitive, percussive clave clicks.

Rather than cruise through each 20-bar part horizontally, let's examine the music in five- and four-bar vertical sections.

Section 1. Because 12 of the melody's 16 bars are played over ♭VI7 (D♭7) and V7 (C7) chords, the music seethes with exotic tension. The melody derives from the F harmonic minor scale, but the ♭VI7/V7 harmony emphasizes the scale's fifth mode, C Phrygian dominant.

The four-bar intro fades in—another Les Paul first?—and introduces the loping mood with a sparse bass-string ostinato and tapped guitar percussion.

In bars 5–8, Guitar 1's ornamented melody is characteristic Paul: hammer-ons, pull-offs, and slides abound. The old-fashioned, foot-powered pump organ harmonizes a third above. The bass and percussion guitar parts, now syncopated to emphasize the "and" of beat *two*, lock into a new 12-bar ostinato. Guitar 2's first response to the melody is an impossibly high C in bar 6.

Ex. 1, Section 1 (bars 1–8)

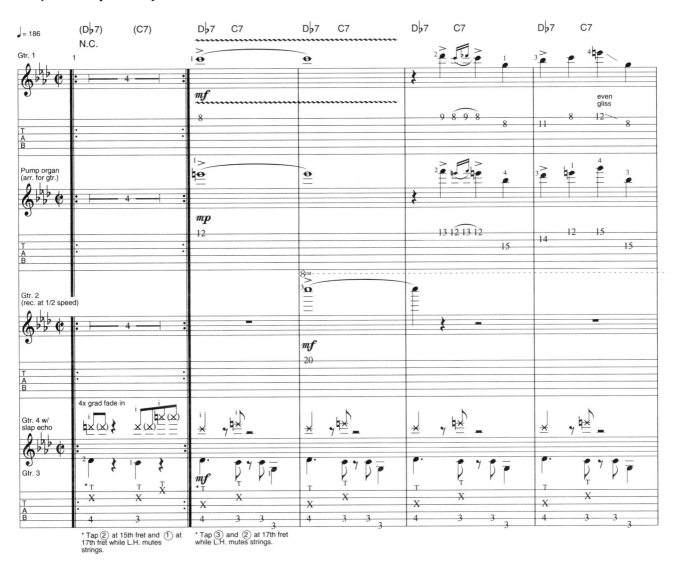

"Caravan" from *Sophisticated Ladies* by Duke Ellington, Irving Mills, and Juan Tizol. © 1937 (renewed 1965) and assigned to Famous Music Corporation and EMI Mills Music Inc. in the USA. Rights for the world outside the USA controlled be EMI Mills Music Inc. (Publishing) and Warner Bros. Publications U.S., Inc. (Print). International copyright secured. All rights reserved.

Section 2. Bars 9–12 begin with the melody (Guitar 1) and harmony (pump organ) sustaining tied whole-notes. Below, Guitar 2 does a double-time dance: After a quick chromatic approach to beat *three*'s D♭, Paul launches a C Phrygian dominant run.

Check out the note sequencing that occurs in Guitar 2, bars 9 (beats *three* and *four*) and 10 (beat *one*): Each downbeat alternates twice with its lower-neighbor scale tone. The downbeat notes combine to form a diminished-7th arpeggio one half-step above the V7 chord—a surefire recipe for altered-dominant sounds.

Ex. 1, Section 2 (bars 9–12)

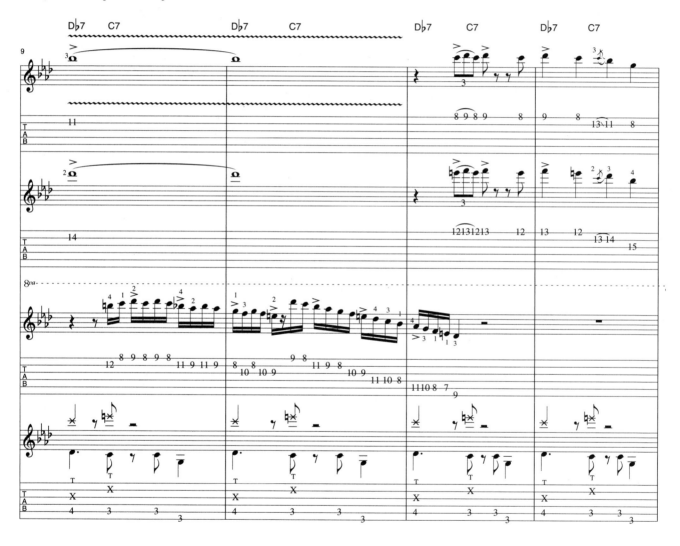

Section 3. Guitar 2's excursion in bars 13-16 is another mind-blowing half-speed recording. From an ascending *C* major arpeggio, Paul grabs the ♭9 (*D♭*) and then works down through the *C* Phrygian dominant scale to *G* (bar 13). His anticipated slide up to the 12th-fret *E* sets off a chain of three ascending-diminished/descending-chromatic motifs (bar 14).

Guitar 1 and the organ resume active duty in bars 15 and 16. Paul animates the melody by giving his patented descending chromatic triplets a 16th-note twist.

Ex. 1, Section 3 (bars 13–16)

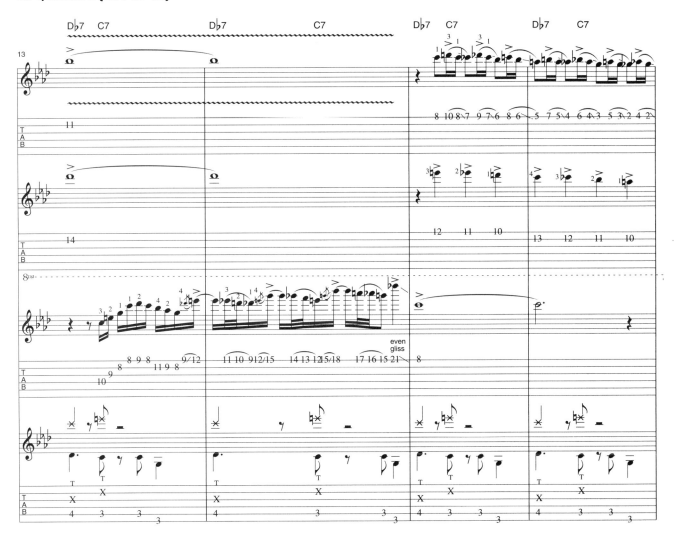

Section 4. At bar 17, the progression finally resolves to four measures of the tonic, *Fm*. Notice how only one note changes in the bass part: *G* drops to *F*. Guitar 2's final fill is a sly quote from Edvard Grieg's "In the Hall of the Mountain King." The pump organ lays out while Guitar 1 adds a cool touch of harmonic ambiguity via the *D–Ab* tritone that functions as *Fm6*.

Ex. 1, Section 4 (bars 17–20)

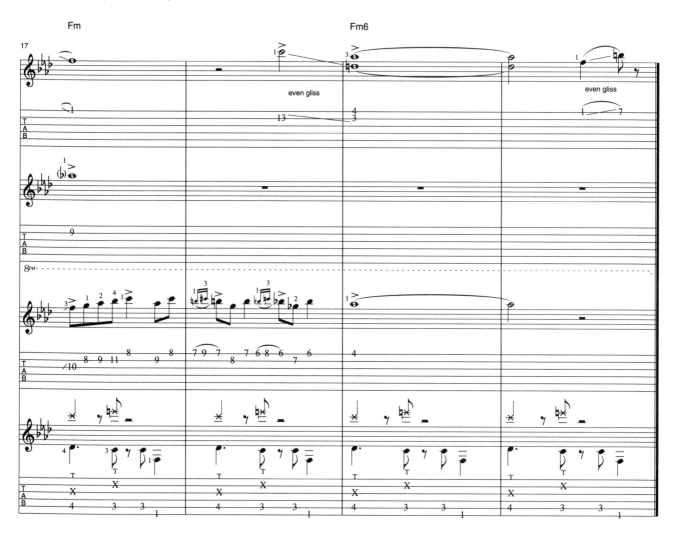

Round two. At this point, the 16-bar theme essentially repeats with Guitar 2 supplying a fistful of new fills. This second time around, Paul restates the super-high *C* one beat earlier before launching a new barrage of countermelodies also recorded at half-speed:

• In bars 9-11, Guitar 2's augmented triads and zippy broken major 3rds move in whole-tones (**Ex. 2**).

Ex. 2

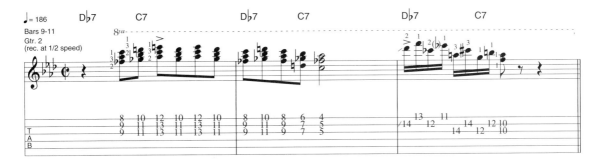

• In bars 13-15, Guitar 2's greased-lightning triplets consist of displaced unison *C*'s played on adjacent strings (**Ex. 3**). In the following measure, Paul pedals off the *C*, alternating slides into *D* and *E*. **Example 4** shows how Paul adapts this idea to the tonic *Fm* in bars 17–20. This phrase climaxes with a pair of out-of-this-world glissandi an octave *above* the 18th and 20th frets.

Ex. 3

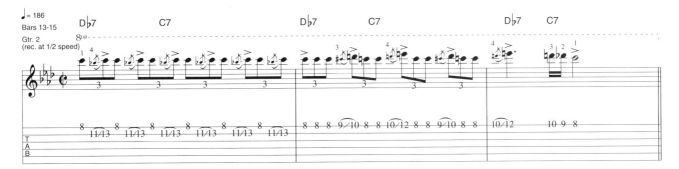

Ex. 4

Example 5 is Guitar 1's alternate take on the melody in bars 15–18. Notice how Paul hammers each double-stopped 4th into a 5th, then pulls off again. The triplets descend chromatically until they reach their target at the 1st fret. Want to make this lick work for you? Simple: Just count the number of beats preceding your target and start the lick that number of frets higher. You're guaranteed a direct hit every time.

Special thanks to Les Paul, Marilyn and Vinnie Bell, Paul Nowinski, Tom Doyle, Christopher Lentz, and T.J. McGann.

Ex. 5

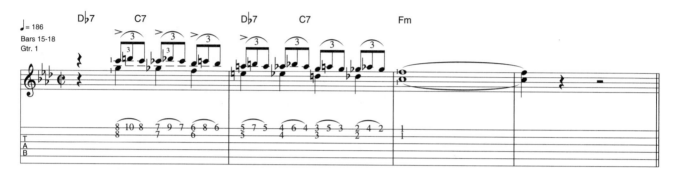

Style Lesson
Cliff's Notes

Cliff Gallup as Taught by Jeff Beck

Originally published in Guitar Player, *April 1993.*

Santa showed up on December 17, 1992, in a FedEx truck. He bestowed two cassettes on me, and I spent the next 90 minutes writhing (yes, *writhing*) to the sounds of Jeff Beck's return to action. New Beck is always rejuvenating, and man, I felt like a fuzzy 13-year-old with his first copy of *Truth*. As different as night and day, *Crazy Legs*, Beck's loving tribute to Gene Vincent and His Blue Caps, and *Frankie's House*, the soundtrack to a hard-hitting, Vietnam-era war film co-written with Jed Leiber, are both major guitar events. Let's savor some tidbits from each.

Beck remains fairly faithful to the Gene Vincent tunes he covers on *Crazy Legs*, and "Race with the Devil" and "Cruisin'" are near-exact recreations of Blue Caps guitarist Cliff Gallup's original performances. In these solos, you can hear many of the ideas and techniques that have become staples of Beck's vocabulary, including pulled-off triplets, slurred and raked gracenotes, vibrato-bar scoops, and chromatically ascending octaves.

Doused with slap echo, the intro and verse rhythm figures from "Race with the Devil" (**Ex. 1**) begin with a muted, low-register riff before sliding into *E6/9* chord breaks. The descending approach to the IV chord (*A7*) uses 6/9 voicings stripped down to just three notes on the upper strings. Each is attacked with an upstroke that precedes a slide into the next chord. The sax-like motif played over the IV chord reappears, transposed, over the I chord before Beck and Gallup head up to the seventh position. Here, what *sounds* like a Travis-picked *B7* chord is actually a pair of descending-6th shapes on the first and third strings.

Ex. 1

"Race With The Devil"

Fast ♩ = 204

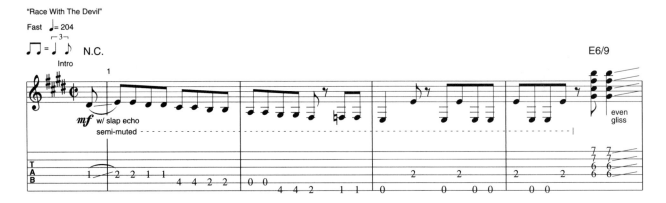

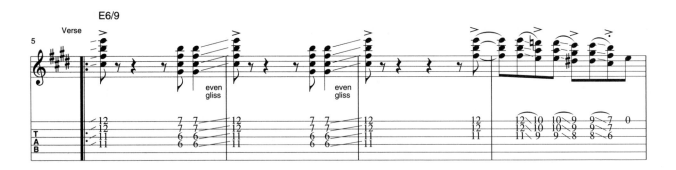

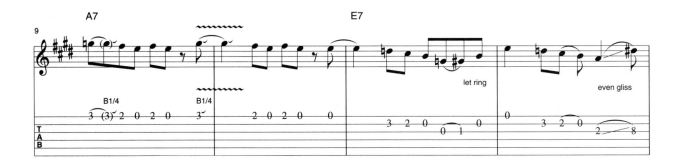

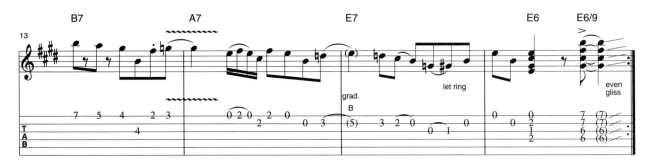

"Race with the Devil" by Gene Vincent © 1956 (renewed 1984) Beechwood Music Corp. All rights reserved.
International copyright secured. Used by permission.

Jeff's rendition of Cliff's first solo (**Ex. 2**) begins with two bars of triplet pull-offs in the twelfth position, where most of the action takes place. A chromatic approach to *C#*, the 3rd of *A7*, precedes double-stop riffing over the IV chord. The two-bar V–IV lick, a series of chromatically ascending octaves on the second and fifth strings, is phrased in a syncopated, three-against-four rhythm.

Ex. 2

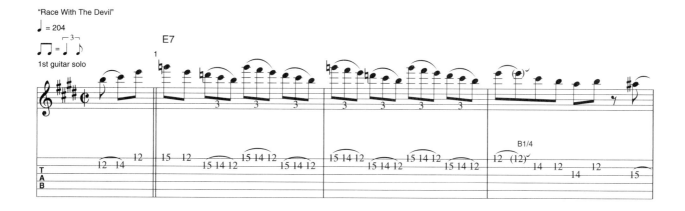

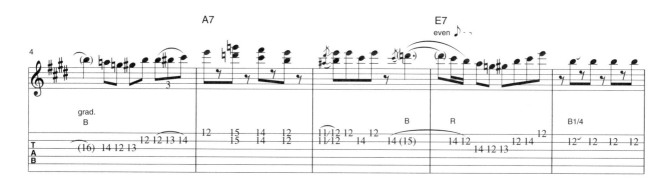

A half-step modulation to *F* shifts the tune into overdrive for the second solo (**Ex. 3**). Two bars of first-position riffing pave the way for a quick leap up the *E* string, but instead of sliding directly to the high *F*, both Gallup and Beck pause on the 12th-fret *E* for a beat. Intentional or not, it sounds cool as hell! Subtle Bigsby-bar bends follow, including bar-scooped double-stops that anticipate the downbeats by eighth-notes and heavy metal by 20 years.

Ex. 3

* distance of bend measured on B string

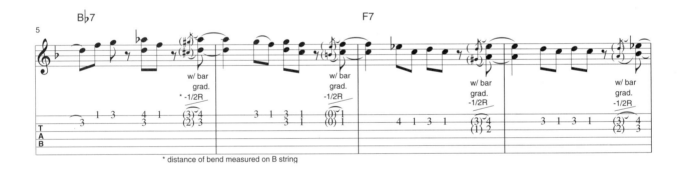

The two-bar ending lick in **Ex. 4** sets up the final chord—a lush *F6/9* crammed into the fourteenth position. A quirky turnaround used throughout "Red Blue Jeans" functions as the ending riff in **Ex. 5**.

Ex. 4

Ex. 5

The rhythm figure to "Cruisin'" (**Ex. 6**) is a fast 16-bar progression. Note how Gallup and Beck imply the *C9* and *D9* chords with triads that can also be seen as *Gm* and *Am*. Also notable is the third-position *G5* chord that includes the open *G* string—a Beck trademark.

Ex. 6

Sandwiched between two equally great "Cruisin'" solos, the 12-bar chorus in **Ex. 7** features a slew of Beck-*cum*-Gallupisms, including gnarly minor-2nd slurs, dissonant minor-2nd double-stops that combine fretted pitches with adjacent open strings, and cascading open-string triplet pull-offs *à la* Les Paul. Though the *F#*'s and *C#*'s reside outside the *G7* tonality, the sheer momentum of the final lick makes them work. Beck used similar ideas throughout the Yardbirds' classic "Jeff's Boogie."

Ex. 7

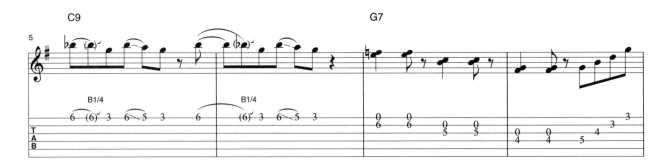

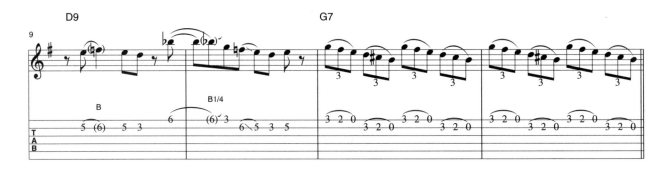

Frankie's House gives Beck plenty of space to stretch out. The music of Thailand and Vietnam influenced the koto-like inflections of **Ex. 8**, where Jeff combines staccato notes with pre-bends and quick grace-note releases. (You can also get this effect by pulling up on the vibrato bar or flipping it around 180 degrees and playing reversed grace-note scoops while you hammer notes with your fretting hand.) The southeast Asian ambience is enhanced with a bluesy vibe in **Ex. 9**.

Ex. 8

Ex. 9

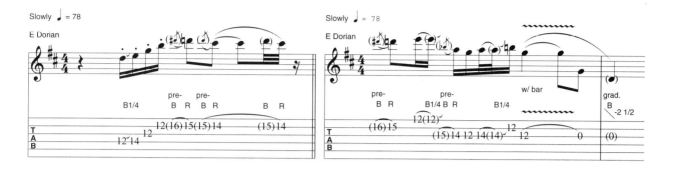

While "Hi-Heel Sneakers" from *Frankie's House* features a bona fide bottleneck solo, Jeff continues to confound listeners with his astonishing faux-slide technique. His subtle vibrato-bar action and fretting-hand bends can also conjure convincing harmonica or sax sounds. Beck puts a unique spin on each note in **Ex. 10**, using only bends to slur between pitches. **Example 11**'s first two bends are played with the bar before resorting to a traditional bend to the tonic E. The bar bends are notated using positive or negative fractions and numerals in half-step increments.

Ex. 10

Ex. 11

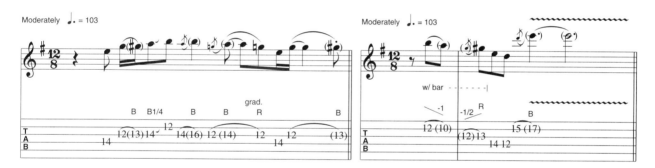

Bars 2 and 3 in **Ex. 12** combine bar scoops with simultaneous finger bends for a convincing bottleneck simulation.

Ex.12

Example 13 recalls a classic Little Walter harmonica lick. Jeff flats the 5th (*B*) with subtle bar dips, and there's Beck stuff smeared all over the short phrase on beat *four*.

Ex.13

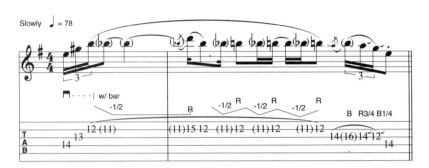

Example 14 is a syncopated "son of 'Rice Pudding'" riff laced with heavy bar scoops. For extra sickness, milk those bar releases for all they're worth.

Ex.14

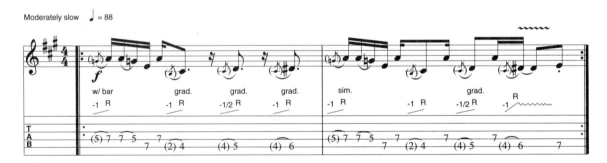

Solo Transcription
Jimi Hendrix
"All Along the Watchtower"

Originally published in Guitar Player, *May 2001.*

Jimi Hendrix's highest-charting U.S. single, "All Along the Watchtower," may be the best Hendrix song Bob Dylan ever wrote. In the liner notes to the 1993 reissue of *Electric Ladyland* [MCA], Hendrix was quoted describing his unique relationship with Dylan's music: "Sometimes I do a Dylan song, and it seems to fit me so right that I figure maybe *I* wrote it."

Crafting guitar parts that became as integral as Dylan's lyrics, Hendrix made the song his own. And while it's rare for a song-writer to favor another artist's arrangement over his own, Dylan said in the same *Electric Ladyland* liner notes, "Ever since [Hendrix] died, I've been doing 'All Along the Watchtower' the way he did it. When I sing it, I always feel like it's a tribute to him."

Before diving into our "Watchtower" transcription, tune down a half-step to match the recording. All pitches in the transcribed examples sound one half-step lower than written.

Guest guitarist Dave Mason's heavily compressed acoustic figure opens the tune with one of the most infamous "Where's the downbeat?" intros of all time. (To this day, I have to struggle not to hear the intro as starting on beat *four*.) **Example 1** illustrates how this deceptive rhythm part begins with a B chord on the "and" of beat *three*, while the C#m and A chords are anticipated on the "and" of *four*. The open first string adds a lustrous shimmer to Mason's C#m and A voicings.

Ex.1

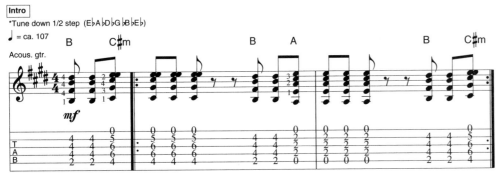

Hendrix's four-bar intro solo (**Ex. 2**) is one of the most memorable and singable guitar solos in rock history. Poised in the twelfth-position C♯ minor pentatonic box, he immediately breaks out with four exquisitely bent 9ths that give you the sense that something extraordinary is happening. Just as unusual is the A chord's targeted 6th in bar 2. Hendrix enters familiar ninth-position C♯ blues territory in bar 3, but he twists it with a hammered 6th in bar 4. His rhythmic momentum prevents any harmonic conflict between this A♯ note and the A in the chord ringing behind it. All four bars of this solo utilize variations on the rhythmic motif from Ex. 1.

Because I got used to hearing Mason's intro rhythmically backwards—with the beat turned around—I heard Hendrix's intro solo backwards as well. Not surprisingly, the solo sounds fantastic either way—the hallmark of a great melody. If you haven't experienced this phenomenon, try moving the bar lines in Ex. 2 back one eighth-note. Cool, huh? (What's that? Now *you* hear it backwards? Oops, sorry about that.)

Ex. 2

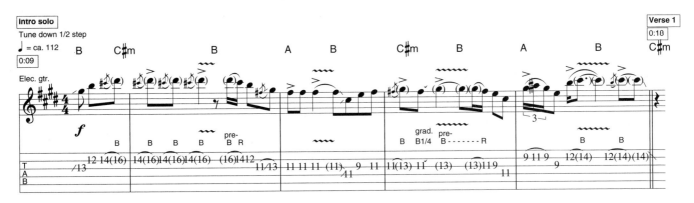

Hendrix's next solo (**Ex. 3**) comes after the song's first verse, and every note here is a high point. With mercurial phrasing, Hendrix shuttles between ninth- and twelfth-position C♯ minor pentatonic boxes for the unison tonic bends in bar 1, another bent 9th in bar 3, one-and-a-half-step bends in bars 4 and 5, and the bluesy burst of brilliance in bars 7 and 8—still one of my favorite Hendrix licks.

Except for an initial on-the-downbeat *C#m* at the beginning of this passage, Mason reverts to his intro rhythm figure.

Ex. 3

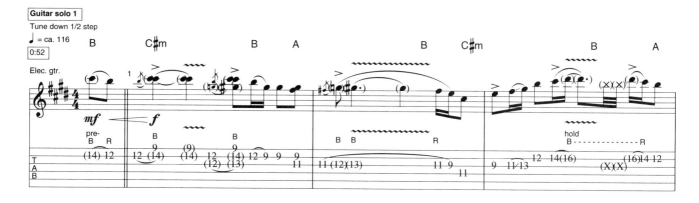

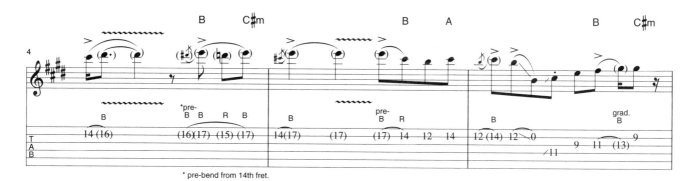

* pre-bend from 14th fret.

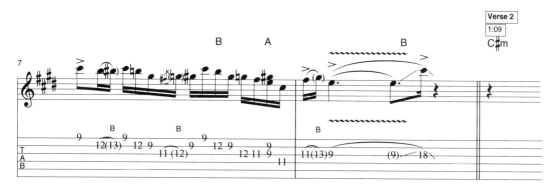

"All Along the Watchtower" words and music by Bob Dylan © 1968, 1985 Dwarf Music. International copyright secured. All rights reserved. Reprinted by permission.

Hendrix's 32-bar, post-second-verse solo (Examples 4a–4d) is composed of four distinct eight-bar movements:

- A second "straight" electric solo (bars 1–8)
- A spacey slide-guitar interlude (bars 9–16)
- A climactic wah solo (bars 17–24)
- A barrage of partial chords, wild fills, and substitutions that dance around the basic progression (bars 25–32)

In bars 1–8 (**Ex. 4a**), Mason's rhythm accents shift; *C#m* and *A* land on beat *one*, and *B* drops on the "and" of beat *three*. Hendrix lays down some funky syncopated rhythms that echo his own Motown-style bass playing. The bent 9th used in the first two solos plays a prominent role in the lick that wraps up bars 7 and 8. Again this all happens between the ninth and twelfth positions, and it's all singable.

Ex. 4a

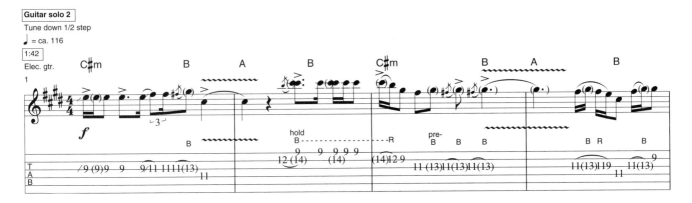

At 1:59, Hendrix breaks into a hallucinatory dream sequence that still sends the senses reeling (**Ex. 4b**). It has been well documented that he played this slide solo with a Zippo lighter, and my guess is he did it on an electric—or amped-up acoustic—12-string. Listen, and you'll hear octaves on all of the single notes in bars 10–16. Long-delay tape echoes add to the overall trippy ambiance. And

there's *another* rhythm guitar shift in this section. Now, every other *B* chord is played on the "and" of beat *three*.

Ex. 4b

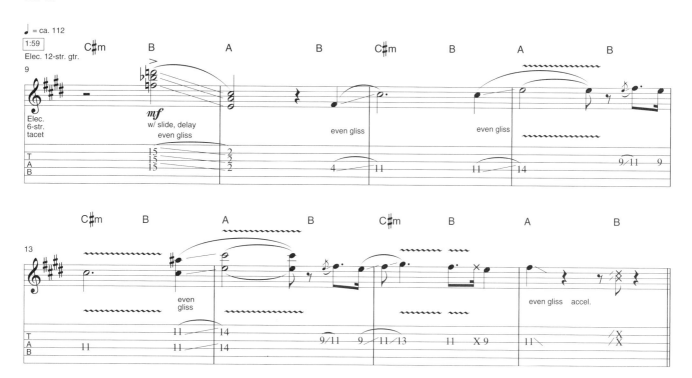

Sporting killer 6-string tone at 2:16 (**Ex. 4c**), Hendrix contrasts his previous spacescape with wah-wah and delay-effected octaves that climb *C#* minor pentatonic from the ♭3rd to the ♭7th (bars 17 and 18). His wah-pumping action settles into a steady eighth-note pulse with a few tone-sculpting exceptions. He churns stream-of-consciousness 16th-note lines in bars 19, 21, and 22, and climaxes with ascending unison bends in bars 23 and 24.

Mason's acoustic rhythm all but disappears beneath Hendrix's eight-bar chordal onslaught in bars 25–32 (**Ex. 4d**). Outlining the progression in diads and triads, Hendrix adds R&B-approved 9ths to the *C#m* and *B* chords, but his *Em*, *F#m*, and *Am* moves over the *A* chords in bars 26 and 30 are from Venus. Baffled by these "mystery chords" for years, I eventually traced their origin to the second- and third-string minor-3rd shapes common to the eighth-position *A* minor pentatonic, tenth-position *A* major pentatonic, and twelfth-position *A* minor pentatonic boxes.

The solo peaks with the kind of rapid-fire ascending unison bends that would mark Edward Van Halen's playing a decade later, and it ends with a frantic trill at the end of bar 32. Though I've been listening to—and playing—this song for years, Hendrix's closing trill was a detail that had eluded my ears. Even 35 years after he left us, Jimi Hendrix is still full of surprises.

Ex. 4c

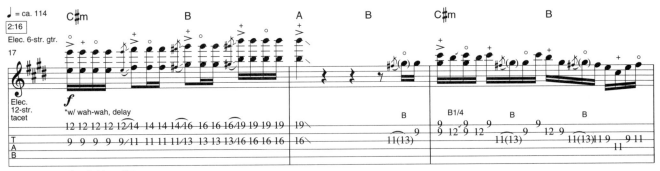

* + = treble position
  o = bass position

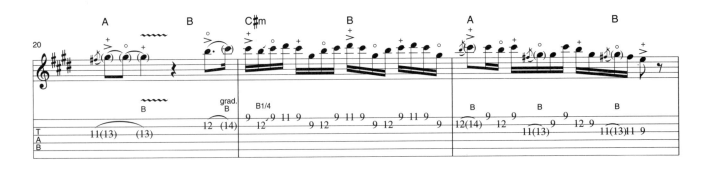

Ex. 4d

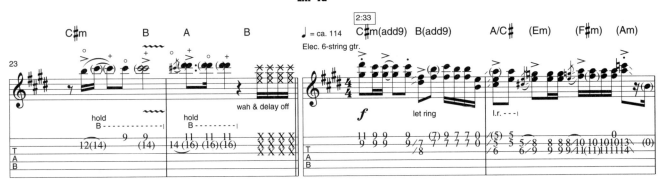

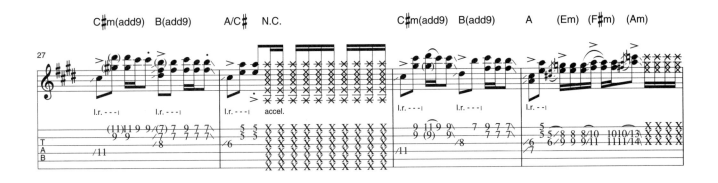

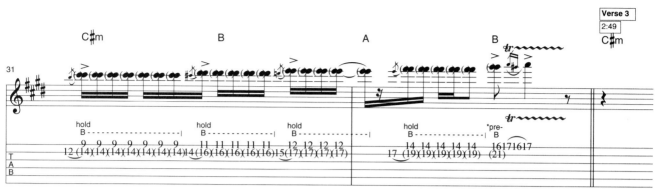

* pre-bend from 19th fret.

Screamin' & Cryin'

Muddy's Blues Taught by Johnny Winter

Originally published in Guitar Player, *March 1994.*

In a world newly exposed to Muddy Waters via TV commercials, tribute albums, and memorial concerts, Johnny Winter remains a rightful keeper of the flame. Winter's lifelong promotion of Muddy's music began when he first heard it on the radio in the '50s, and it continues to this day.

In the mid '70s Johnny befriended the master bluesman, producing and playing on his highly acclaimed last four albums. Johnny brought Muddy back to his Chicago roots; eschewing modern, sterile studio techniques, he recorded the entire band live, primarily through a single ambient room mike. The Grammy-winning results boosted Waters' popularity in his final years, and Muddy came to regard Johnny as a son. Johnny's love for Muddy was evident when he enthusiastically accepted our invitation to discuss his mentor's music.

I think those four albums you did with Muddy will have as much historical significance as his 1941 plantation recordings.

They were really important to me, because I'd always idolized Muddy and learned so much from listening to his records. It was one of my biggest musician experiences just to get to know the guy. I *still* learn so much from his records.

I don't like it that I'm getting this old! So many of my friends, the people I learned from, aren't here now. In another ten years or so *I'm* gonna be one of the elder guys. I like having the older guys to look up to. I'd rather be a student than a teacher!

FREE Audio Version Online
www.GuitaRev.TrueFire.com

You've already been a teacher to many.

I guess it goes in a circle. You learn from people, and then, if you do it long enough and do it right, people start learning stuff from you.

Did you try to learn Muddy's style note-for-note?

At first I would learn it that way, but then I would start putting my own little things in there.

Muddy's style was much sparser than yours.

That was always my trouble with just playing a legitimate Muddy Waters song. It was always hard for me to be that sparse and lay back that much. He could do it even if it was just one guitar. And it didn't make any difference whether it was just him—it sounded great!

Sometimes the art of restraint is the hardest of all.

Boy, is it, especially for me! I just don't feel it that way. I always feel like putting another note in there. When I've been listening to a lot of Muddy's music, I can play it exactly, but if I haven't heard it for a while, it kind of goes into Johnny Winter.

How was Muddy's guitar set up?

He used heavy strings, and his action was way up there. I don't know how he played regular guitar. In fact, I remember him telling me one time, "You know, playing somebody else's guitar is just like stealing their woman. If she don't wanna be with you, it's just like saying, 'Let go of me, man! I ain't yours.' Pick up that guitar, and it tells you right away, 'You shouldn't be messin' with me!'"

Did he always use a bottleneck for slide?

He always used that little slide that didn't cover too many strings. In the old days he probably used the bottle.

Could you recall some of the first Muddy licks you learned?

The first ones I remember were two different intros. Now, this isn't exactly the way that Muddy did it later on, because I'm in E tuning, but he used to play this a lot [*plays **Ex. 1** and **Ex. 2**]:*

Ex. 1

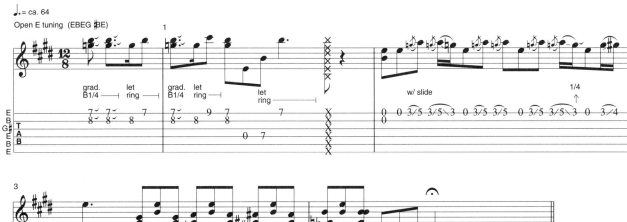

Ex. 2

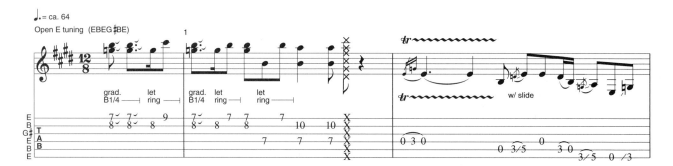

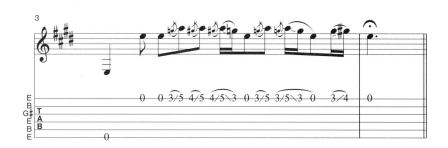

Sometimes, though, he'd just play this [*plays **Ex. 3***]:

Ex. 3

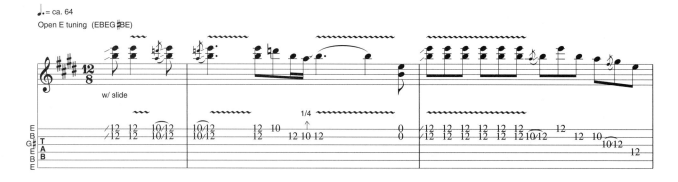

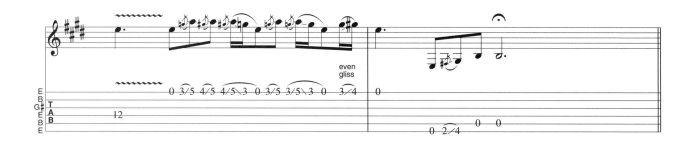

A lot of times on the old records you'd hear that open string ring, so I'm sure he must have tuned to an open *E* on his first records. You didn't hear that sound on his later records. In the early period he also did a lot in open *A* or open *G* [*plays* **Ex. 4**].

Ex. 4

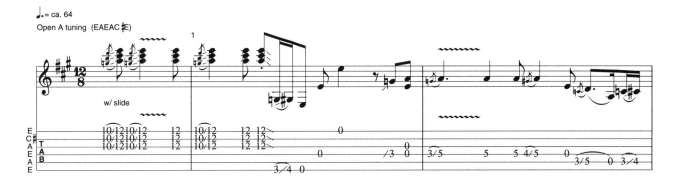

That's a little Johnny comin' out there [*laughs*]! But Muddy would do something more like this [*plays* **Ex. 5**]:

Ex. 5

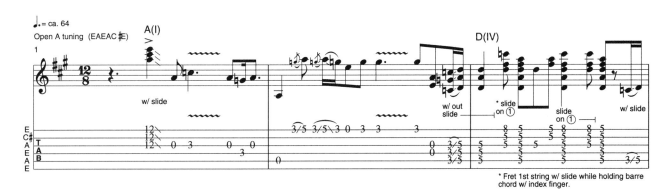

* Fret 1st string w/ slide while holding barre chord w/ index finger.

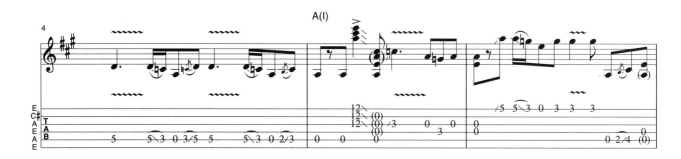

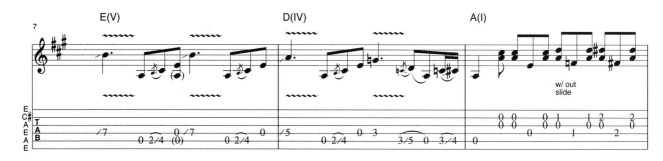

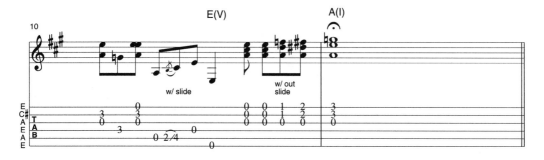

He had a period where I don't know how many of his songs had pretty much the same leads [plays **Ex. 6** and **Ex. 7**]:

Ex. 6

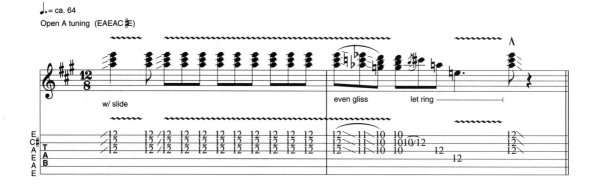

Ex. 7

When people adapt Muddy's songs, they seem to focus on one little riff and develop it into their own thing. How did you adapt "Rollin' and Tumblin'"?

There's so much to focus on! I just heard "Rollin' and Tumblin'" last night. It was the old version with Baby Face Leroy, and I thought, "Man, that is just the wildest thing I've ever heard!" That version was just so cool that I had to try to get some of that wildness in there [*plays **Ex. 8** and **Ex. 9***].

Ex. 8

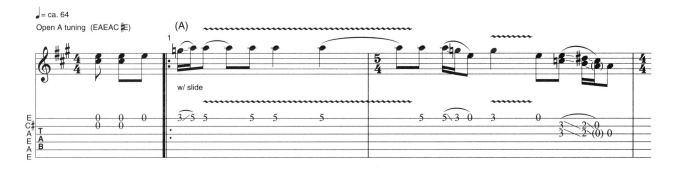

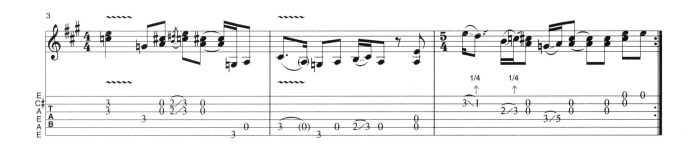

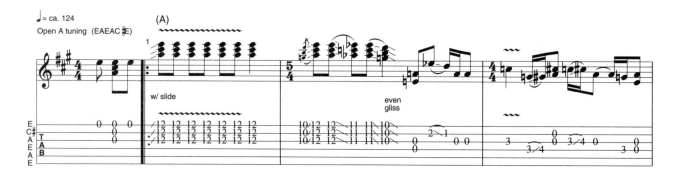

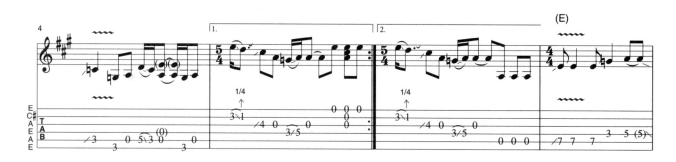

Did Muddy always play in an open tuning?

In the last part of his life he tuned regular, and whatever key he wanted to be in, he'd just put the capo there. Bob Margolin [Waters' guitarist during his final years] would leave guitars around in open tuning, and he said Muddy would pick them up and could still play that way, but he just kind of stopped doing it. Neither of us knew exactly why—you couldn't push Muddy too far, you know? If he didn't want to talk about it, he'd just say, "Well, I just don't have enough guitars," or make up some excuse, and that was it. You couldn't keep bugging him about it. But both of us wanted to see him do that move, because he played so much of the open-*A* or open-*G* stuff in the old days. It was kind of a shame to see him stop.

Did Muddy have a sense of his own greatness?

He'd always say, "I'm not much of a guitar player—so-and-so plays better than I do." Sometimes he'd sound like he was putting himself down, but I think he knew. He knew how much soul he had.

Style Lesson

Soaring with Skydog

The Duane Allman Style

Originally published in Guitar Player, *October 1993.*

Thirty-four years after his passing, Duane Allman remains the unsurpassed king of electric slide guitar. Already steeped in the blues of Muddy, Wolf, Willie Dixon, B.B. King, Clapton, and Beck, Duane became enamored with slide after hearing the late Jesse Ed Davis perform Blind Willie McTell's "Statesboro Blues" with Taj Mahal at an L.A. club. Using a glass bottle for a slide, Duane also began emulating Little Walter, Sonny Boy Williamson, and other blues harmonica players. In time, even his non-slide playing took on characteristics of his bottleneck style, as if both were becoming welded into one voice.

Duane was obviously a fast learner with an uncanny grasp of open-*E* tuning, as heard on his records with the Allman Brothers Band and his soulful backing of Wilson Pickett, Aretha Franklin, King Curtis, John Hammond, Boz Scaggs, Clarence Carter, and others. Though he began playing bottleneck in standard tuning, Allman preferred the advantages of open *E*, and he eventually limited his standard-tuned slide excursions to songs like "Dreams" and "Mountain Jam."

Early in 1970 the Brothers cut a studio version of "Statesboro Blues" in the key of *C*, while the later live *At Fillmore East* version was in *D*. A few months later, during the recording of *Idlewild South*, Allman tracked more cutting-edge, open-*E*-tuned electric slide on "Don't Keep Me Wonderin'" and "One More Ride." Continuing his session work, he began to hit his stride later that year during Eric Clapton's *Layla* sessions. His bottleneck ranged from subdued to incendiary on eight of these tracks, almost all of which are in open *E* ("Layla" and "I Am Yours" are the exceptions). The *Layla* outtake "Mean Old World," a dobro duet with EC, is perhaps Duane's only recording in the more rural open-*G* tuning. Duane's next big project, the Brothers' *At Fillmore East*, represents the pinnacle of bottleneck performance—*the* book of electric slide.

FREE Audio Version Online
www.GuitaRev.TrueFire.com

Gear-wise, Duane favored Les Pauls, 50-watt Marshalls, and a glass Coricidin bottle worn over his ring finger. While sliding, he used his right-hand thumb, index, and middle fingers, which served double duty damping unwanted strings. Duane also used his left-hand middle and index fingers to damp behind the bottle. Low frets and medium-high action were also helpful. For accuracy like Duane's, align the tip of your ring finger directly over the fret.

Guitarists commonly use bends, hammer-ons, pull-offs, and finger slides to get from one note to the next. The slide imposes limitations on these techniques but offers several alternatives. In **Ex. 1a** both notes are fretted with the slide with no audible glissando in between. **Example 1b** features a picked grace-note slide into the second note, a motion performed with a single pick attack in **Ex. 1c**. Think blues harp for the even gliss in **Ex. 1d**. The grace-note slide preceding the first note of each previous example adds even more smoky harmonica flavor.

Ex. 1a–d

The advantages of open-*E* tuning are increased string tension (for more sustain) and economy of motion. Raising the open fifth and fourth strings a whole-step and the third string a half-step produces an open *E* chord (**Ex. 2a**), giving you, from low to high, the root, 5th, root, 3rd, 5th, and root. Since the root positions on the sixth and first strings remain unaffected, it's not necessary to relearn notes when moving the chord shape around the fingerboard. Using the slide to barre all six strings, this chord voicing may be transposed to 11 other fret positions to accommodate chord changes or playing in different keys before recycling an octave higher (**Ex. 2b**). Open-*E* tuning also offers easy access to all three triad inversions, playable as chords or arpeggios. **Example 2c** demonstrates this while summarizing Duane's right-hand technique. For arpeggios, begin with the fingers resting on the strings as if you were about to play the entire chord, and then pluck each note individually.

Ex. 2a–d

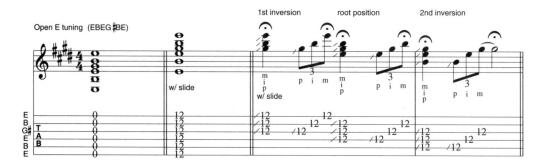

When it came to spinning single-note lines—which comprised 99% of his slide work—Duane preferred the urban "box" approach over more traditional open-string stylings. The box shape is formed by the addition of neighbor tones below the tonic chord position. **Examples 3a** and **3b** illustrate the neighbors (notated below the downward arrow) a whole-step below each chord tone. These lower neighbors (the lowered 7th, 4th, and 2nd/9th) are incorporated in a typical Duane-style lick in **Ex. 3c**.

Ex. 3a–c

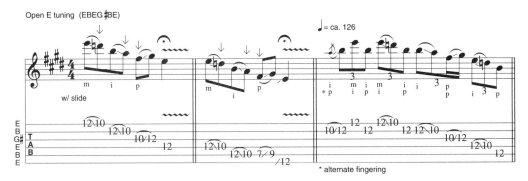

Examples **4a** and **4b** show the chromatic half-step neighbors (the natural 7th, raised 4th/lowered 5th, and lowered 3rd), while **Ex. 4c** adapts them to the previous lick.

Ex. 4a–c

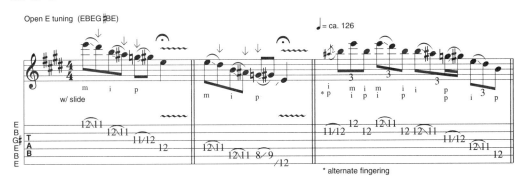

In **Ex. 5** the same lick is treated to a combination of whole-step and chromatic lower neighbors.

Ex. 5

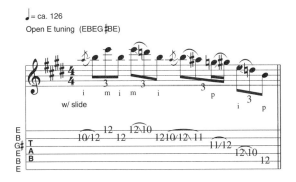

Be sure to explore another important element of Duane's sound, the world of sweet 'n' sour microtones present between neighbor tones. Transpose these ideas over the entire fingerboard. Remember, Duane played equally fluently in any key.

The next few examples cover some of the building blocks of Duane's style. Each motif stands on its own and may be developed in many ways, including repetition, rhythmic displacement, elongation, and retrograde. **Example 6a** features a four-note motif moving across adjacent string groups with whole-step lower neighbors. **Example 6b** shows what a difference a subtle change in phrasing can make.

Ex. 6a

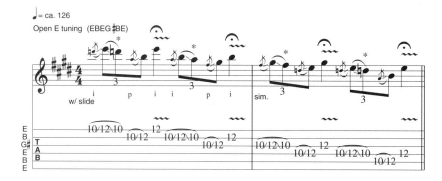

Ex. 6b

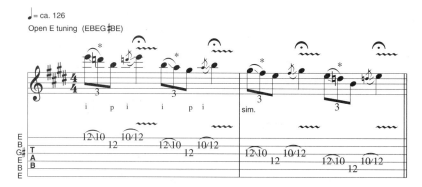

Examples 7a through **7d** follow the same logic using a five-note motif. For some astonishing variations, try replacing the whole-step lower neighbors marked by asterisks with chromatic neighbors or in-between microtones.

Ex. 7a–d

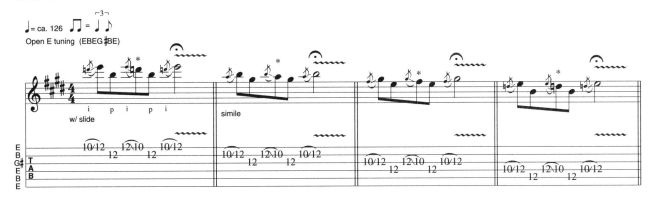

Neighbors *above* the tonic chord include the 2nd/9th, 6th, and 4th. Duane used these sparingly, mostly as grace-note slides or for an occasional splash of pentatonic-major color. Instead, he'd extend the box by momentarily zipping up a major 3rd on the first or fourth strings, or by using the important minor-3rd spacing (found only between the second and third strings) to create a dominant 7th chord fragment three frets above the tonic. In *E*, sliding up three frets from the tonic's *G#* and *B* yields *B* and *D♮*, part of the *E7* chord (**Ex. 8a**). **Example 8b** shows the whole-step and chromatic neighbor possibilities for both two-note structures.

Ex. 8a–b

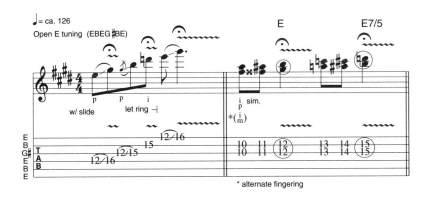

* alternate fingering

Culled from medium-tempo shuffles, **Examples 9a–10b** capture some of Duane's signature phrases. All have been transposed to *E* for mixin' and matchin'. **Example 9a** is very harmonica-like. Add even more sass by exploiting those microtones. **Example 9b** uses the implied 7th chord described above, and then outlines a descending box combining whole- and half-step lower neighbors. **Example 9c**'s chromatically ascending minor 3rds lead up to a signature major-3rd jump up the first string before the descending box/octave-leap conclusion. A similar move in **Ex. 10a** navigates the IV–I change, as does **Ex. 10b**, a funky, mid-register harp-style lick.

Ex. 9a

Ex. 9b

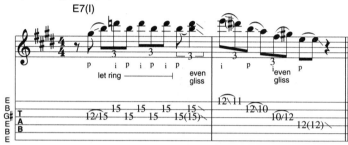

Ex. 9c

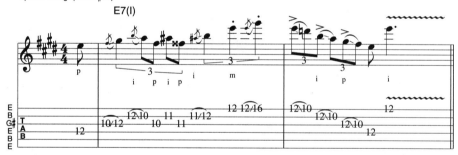

Ex. 10a

Ex. 10b

Transposed to the key of *D*, the blues harp outing in **Ex. 11** covers the last four measures of a 12-bar blues. Duane's flawless intonation is evident as he zips off the fingerboard to the hypothetical 26th fret. Move it up a whole step (to *E*) for a real trip into the stratosphere.

Ex. 11

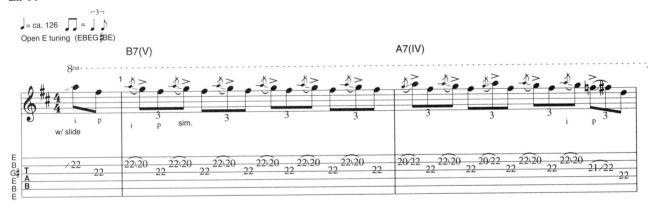

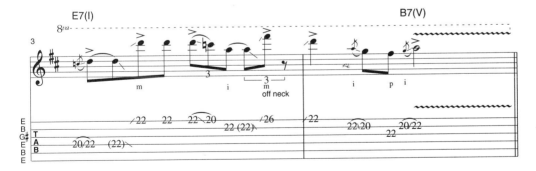

When bottlenecking in standard tuning, Duane often wove adventurous linear excursions up and down the string in place of the blues-box approach, perhaps partially influenced by his interest in jazz greats Miles Davis and John Coltrane. Duane's melodic development is masterful in **Ex. 12**, taken from a videotaped performance of "Dreams." His two-bar call-and-response lines emphasize a 3/4 pulse, while the rhythm section lays down a 6/8 jazz waltz.

Special thanks to brother Jas Obrecht for supplying valuable reference material.

Ex. 12

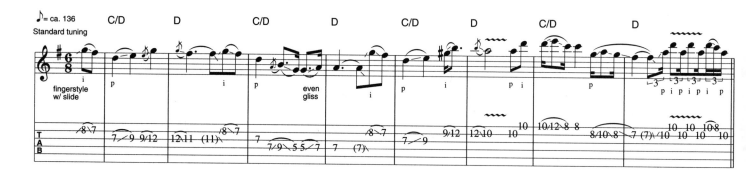

Style Lesson
Classic Carlos
A Portrait of Dorian Un-Gray

Originally published in Guitar Player, *January 1993.*

Carlos Santana personifies the ideal of being emotionally committed to every note. When Santana hit the international scene in 1969 with a sound that combined jazz, blues, rock, and Latin, no one had yet coined that notorious "f" word—fusion. But Carlos' playing sounded totally unlike anything in rock.

Many of Santana's lines are constructed from the usual materials: pentatonic major and minor scales, blues scales, and diatonic modes. (He particularly favors Dorian.) But rhythm may be the most important element of Carlos' playing. If you were to remove the pitches from his melodic lines, the pure rhythms would be as much at home on a conga or timbale as on the guitar. When working out the following examples, try learning the rhythms before adding the notes.

Some aspects of Santana's playing are difficult to translate on paper. His breathy, elastic rhythms often defy accurate notation as they accelerate ahead of or drop slightly behind the beat. One way to get a handle on this "bouncing ball" effect is to practice rhythms in which each successive beat is increased or decreased by one evenly divided accent:

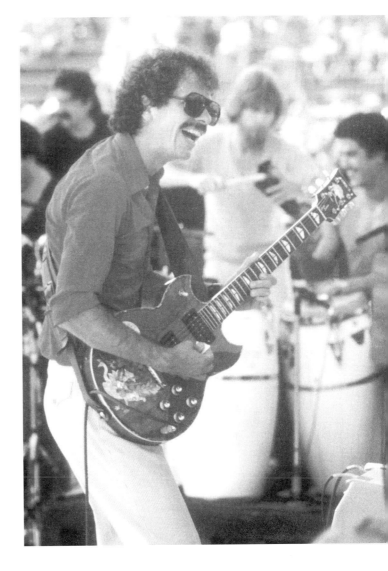

A typical Santana solo—if there is such a thing—might contain blues-drenched call-and-response phrases, unexpected melodic twists colored with intervals outside the pedestrian pentatonic scale,

FREE Audio Version Online
www.GuitaRev.TrueFire.com

syncopated rhythm motives, a tremolo-picked slow glissando moving to a climactic high bend, and perhaps conclude with an infinitely sustained note. (In the live Osaka version of "Europa," Carlos holds one note for 59 seconds!) And, of course, every note drips with that inexplicable *something* that the late music critic Ralph J. Gleason termed the "X factor." Though we can barely scratch the surface, here are a few of Carlos' finest.

Example 1 is one of Santana's most familiar early-period licks. Begin in the tenth position, making sure you milk the release of the first bend for all it's worth. Enhance the heavy Peter Green vibe with a slide into the *E* chord's 9th, which is also the 5th of the Vm chord (*Am*).

Ex. 1

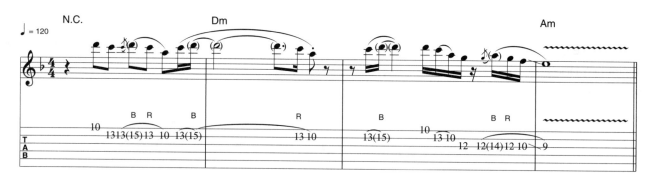

Example 2 begins with a two-bar call-and response phrase ripe with 16th-note syncopations. The phrase repeats and then concludes with a dip to the ♭7 (*C*), eventually returning to the tonic *D* via a lazy quarter-note triplet. This flurry of activity followed by a long sustained resolution is another Santana trademark.

Ex. 2

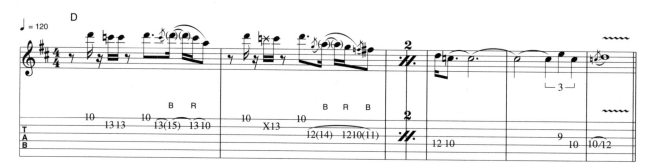

Framed by a signature Im–IV Dorian vamp (*Am-D*), **Ex. 3** finds Santana playing musical question-and-answer between the upper and middle registers of the fifth-position *A* Dorian mode. The half-step slides into the *F#*'s evoke Wes Montgomery and George Benson.

Ex. 3

A combination of ascending bends peppered with dramatic rests and mixed rhythmic group-ings creates a sense of urgency in the opening measure of **Ex. 4**. For the shift back to the twelfth po-sition, play the *F#* at the end of bar 1 with your middle or ring finger so you can comfortably finger the remaining E Dorian/pentatonic minor phrase. The underlying chord progression is built from a harmonized *E* pentatonic minor scale.

Ex. 4

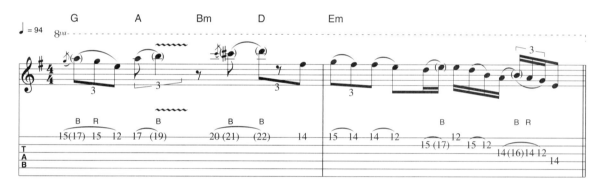

While **Ex. 5**'s sax-like opening figure is derived from the *F* harmonic minor scale, you can also think of it as a *C7* arpeggio played over the *F* Dorian vamp. Bars 2 and 3 superimpose arpeggiated *Eb* and *Bb* major triads, followed by a short B.B. King-ism. Next, two chromatically descending fourths raise the tension. Barre the 16th fret with your 3rd finger and the 15th fret with your 2nd fin-ger to ensure a comfortable arrival at the thirteenth position for the bluesy wrap-up in bar 5.

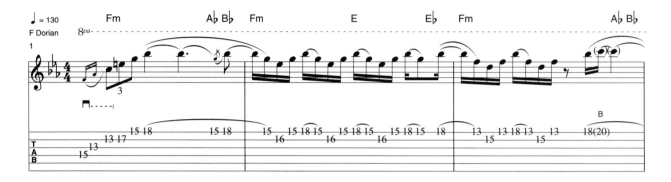

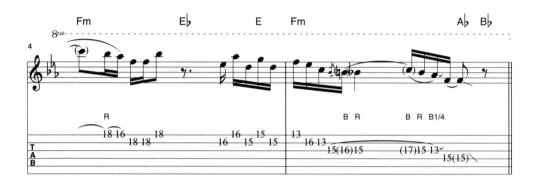

Example 6 exemplifies Santana's Coltrane-infused collaborations with John McLaughlin. Santana opens with a descending *F#* pentatonic minor scale superimposed over a Mixolydian vamp (*A6–B*). Note how these rhythms accelerate, as we discussed earlier. The *D#* alludes to *F#* Dorian (relative to *B* Mixolydian), as do the following pair of broken minor-3rd intervals descending in whole steps. The next minor 3rd descends only a half-step, bringing the ♭5 into the picture for a split second before moving back to *F#* Dorian. The phrase beginning at the end of bar 4 moves from low-register, twelfth position *F#* pentatonic minor to a rapid, 16th-note ascent via *F#* Dorian. A tremolo-picked, even gliss beginning on *F#* peaks with a high bend into *C#*. Extremely hip: the fact that this *C#* and the notes of the closing *F#* pentatonic minor lick are the 9, ♭7, and 5 of the tonic *B*.

Ex. 6

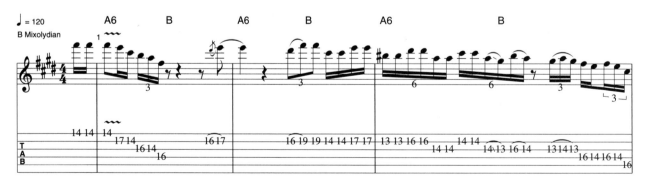

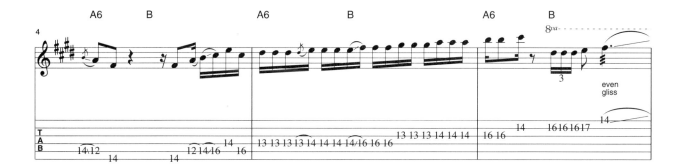

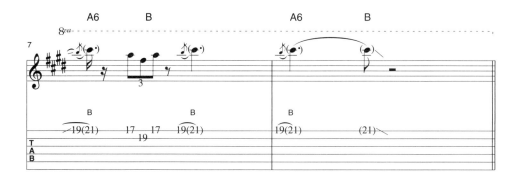

A lush IV–I progression in C (*Fmaj7–Cmaj7*) accompanies **Ex. 7**'s combination of a seventh- and eighth-position *C* major scale and fifth-position *C* major pentatonic (phrased as *A* pentatonic minor). The final two measures offer proof that you don't have to play a lot of notes if you've got a good sense of rhythm.

Ex. 7

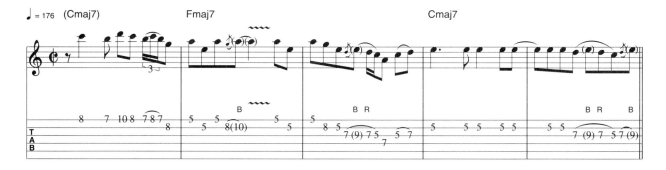

Representative of Santana's work in the '90s, **Ex. 8** offers another lively Im–IV Dorian vamp. Here, in tenth position, he plays a memorable short rhythm motive, rests for three beats, then plays a perfectly executed 16th-note phrase that flows seamlessly into a restatement of the first motive. Note the "mirror image" 16th-note groupings on beats *two* and *three* of bar 2. The concluding lick leans heavily on the 6th (B), a key Dorian ingredient.

Ex. 8

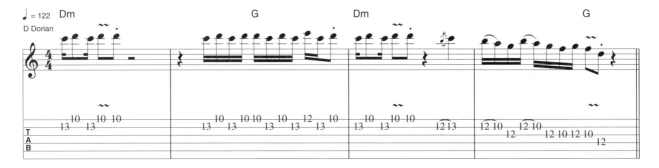

In **Ex. 9**, an oblique bend to the 9th kicks off an *F* Mixolydian excursion that combines Santana's legato stylings and salsa rhythms. After the sustained bends, Carlos hammers and pulls his way down the *B* string to the first position. The extra-hot Mixolydian conclusion contains a beautifully placed 9th (*G*) where one might normally expect to hear the root.

Ex. 9

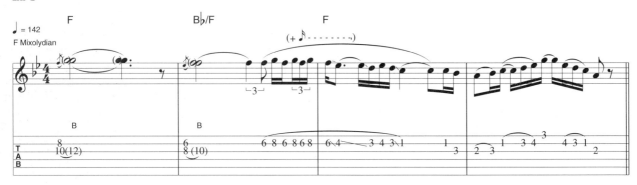

Example 10 shows a more recent variation of the accelerating-rhythm effect, this time using pull-offs. Begin with your 2nd finger (to accommodate the fingering of the final lick) and think "bouncing ball." The unique closing lick combines *E* Dorian and blues scales, and it's just one more reason why we love you, Carlos!

Ex. 10

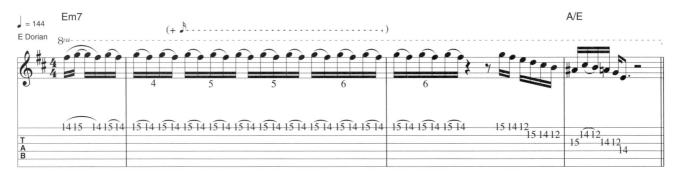

Rock Heart, Blues Soul

The Essential Stevie Ray Vaughan Licks

Originally published in Guitar Player, *December 1993.*

Blend the styles of Albert, B.B., Freddie, and Earl King, T-Bone Walker, Lightnin' Hopkins, Muddy Waters, Hubert Sumlin, Buddy Guy, Otis Rush, Albert Collins, Magic Sam, Guitar Slim, Jimmy Reed, Chuck Berry, Lonnie Mack, Jimi Hendrix, Eric Clapton, Jeff Beck, Peter Green, and Johnny Winter in a musical Cuisinart. Strain through a loving, fertile imagination. What do you get? A lesson in state-of-the-art blues guitar courtesy of the late, great Stevie Ray Vaughan.

Vaughan combined an encyclopedic knowledge of blues phraseology with an uncanny instinct for spontaneous reorganization. He was a true improviser. "He never played it the same way once, much less twice," according to brother Jimmie, who was responsible for teaching Stevie Ray to teach himself.

While SRV soaked up all music like a sponge, he constantly cited Jimi Hendrix as a dominant influence. Jimi's guiding light permeated Stevie Ray's entire repertoire of straight rockers, swinging shuffles, slow blues, R&B rave-ups, and dreamy ballads. It was almost as if he could tap into Hendrix's improvisational spirit and ask, "How might Jimi have played this?" His reinterpretations of Jimi's ideas went far beyond mere imitation; SRV was a legitimate heir to Hendrix.

Like Hendrix, Vaughan relied on an ever-evolving gear setup. But the real key to his tone was Stevie Ray's ability to pull amazing sounds and nuances from the instrument with his hands alone. Always tuned down a half-step (except on the recently released *In the Beginning*), Vaughan opted, unlike Hendrix, for mammoth-sized

www.GuitaRev.TrueFire.com

strings, sometimes sets as extreme as .018–.074. These gave him a larger-than-life sound but also took their toll. He once showed a pair of *Guitar Player* editors how he repaired the divots in his left-hand fingers by applying Super Glue to his right forearm, setting his fingertips in the adhesive, and then ripping the fingers away, sealed with a "skin patch" torn from his arm. I once shook SRV's hand after a performance, and his fingers on both hands were wrapped in blood-soaked bandages—testimony to the commitment he put into every note.

Let's begin our lesson with a look at SRV's rhythm stylings. **Example 1** illustrates a typical Hendrix-influenced figure. The multi-register jumps create a simultaneous rhythm-and-lead effect. Steady your "16th-note clock" and play the example a few dozen times, adding your own variations.

Ex. 1

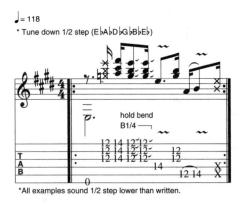

Example 2 surrounds a tonic *E9* with chromatic jabs before concluding with parallel 9th chords. The open-*E* pedal creates the illusion of more than one part. Use alternate picking.

Ex. 2

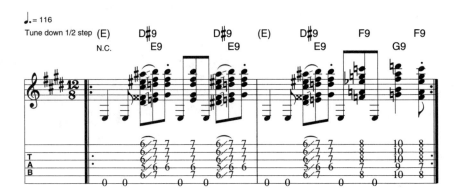

In **Ex. 3**, an uptempo single-note rhythm figure with chordal punctuation, the first two-bar phrase outlines *A7* while the second implies *A7#9* (or *Am7*, for lack of a *C#*). For total authenticity, fret the sixth string with your thumb.

Ex. 3

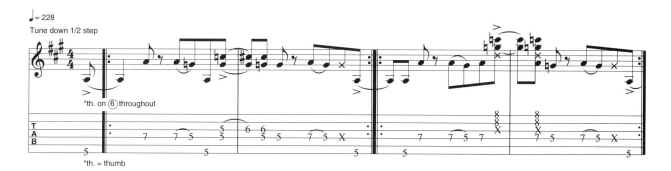

Example 4 combines Hendrixy R&B octaves, double-stop bends, and register leaps before concluding with a cool three-against-four cross-rhythm.

Ex. 4

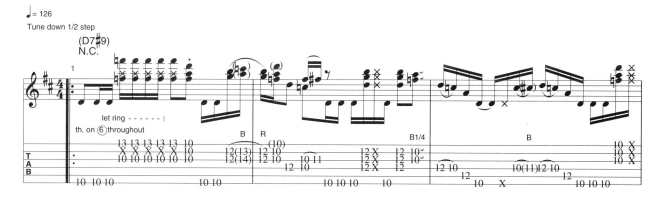

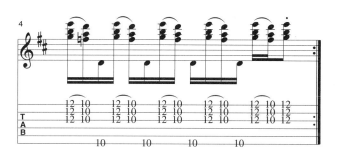

The three-against-four cross-rhythm in **Ex. 5** creates an exciting against-the-grain effect. Since the motif starts halfway through bar 1, it doesn't recycle until the middle of bar 4.

Ex. 5

Played over a V–IV–I progression, **Ex. 6** milks the twelfth-position *E* pentatonic minor box for all it's worth, melding Hendrix and British blues elements.

Ex. 6

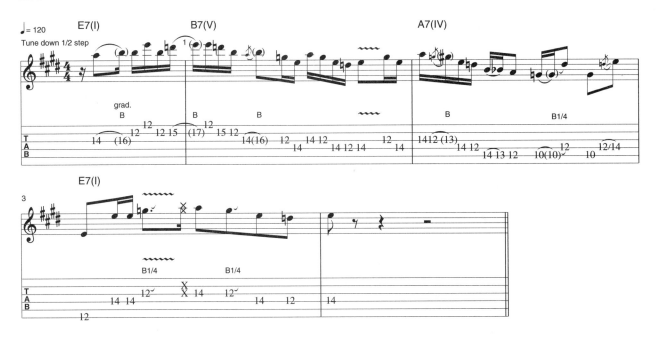

Example 7's opening sweet 'n' sour bends precede a IV-chord phrase that evokes Albert King in bars 2 and 3 and Clapton in bar 4. The Albert-style index-finger bends midway through bar 2 are less than comfy, but the results are worth the pain.

Ex. 7

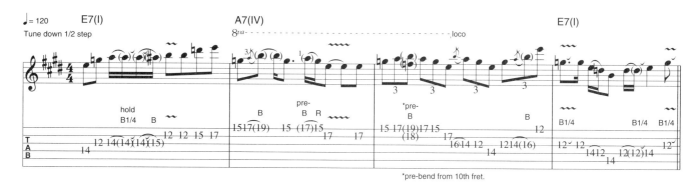

*pre-bend from 10th fret.

A straight-eighth groove similar to Earl King's "Come On, Pt. 1" (covered as "Pt. 2" by Hendrix and "Pt. 3" by SRV) underscores Examples 8, 9, and 10. Chuck Berry–style unison bends open **Ex. 8**. In the third measure SRV shifts into a Hendrix vibe.

Ex. 8

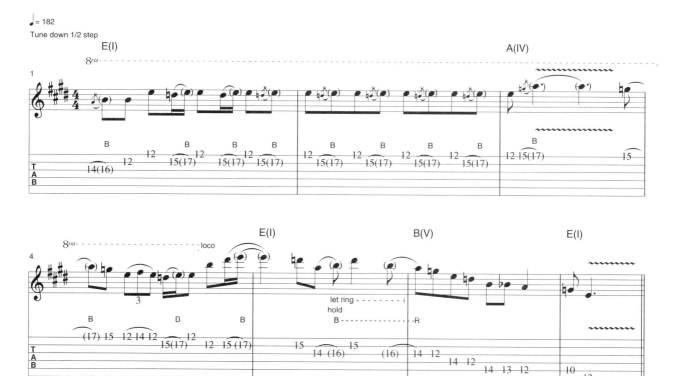

Example 9 emphasizes a three-against-eight rhythm using open-string pedal tones punctuated by octave pull-offs similar to those on Hendrix's "Come On, Pt. 2" solo.

Ex. 9

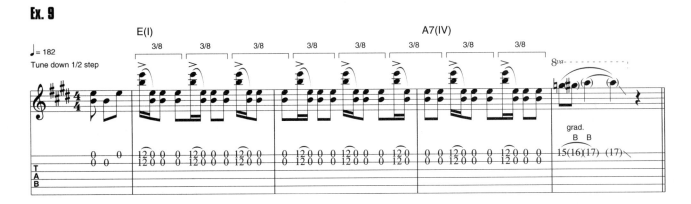

A single pick attack kicks off the legato excursion in **Ex. 10**, which navigates a I–IV progression entirely on the *G* string, another Jimi-ism.

Ex. 10

Example 11 explores some open-position possibilities over the groove to Hendrix's "Voodoo Child (Slight Return)." The flashy, open-string runs illustrate Lonnie Mack's impact on SRV.

Ex. 11

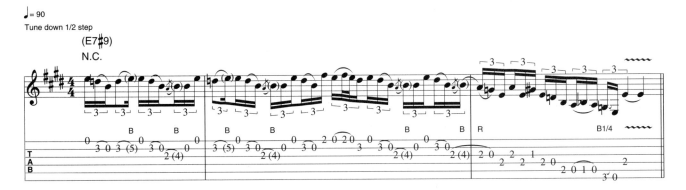

The opening four bars of a 12-bar shuffle, **Ex. 12a** is a mini-ode to Albert King. Play the first bend with your 3rd finger and the second with your 2nd finger, working your way down to the index-finger "dee-dah" lick. The partially released bend halfway through bar 4 adds a typical bitter-sweet touch. **Example 12b** covers the IV–I change with a subtle mixture of straight and swung eighth-notes. (The *B♭* over the IV chord is something you don't hear too often.) The V–IV–I–V progression in Ex. 12c completes the 12-bar form. Listen closely—you'll hear echoes of practically every-one cited in the opening paragraph.

Ex. 12a

Ex. 12b

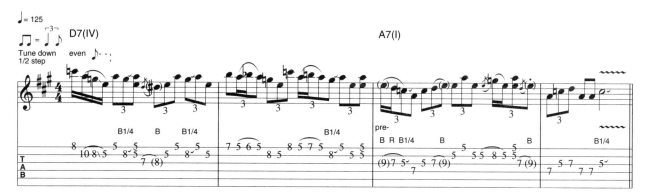

Ex. 12c

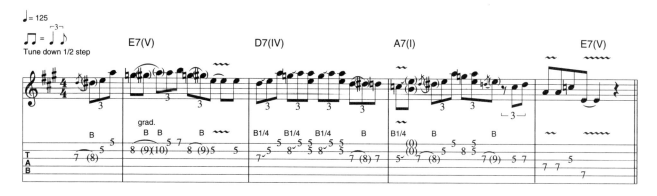

Example 13a confirms Vaughan's love of jazz organ trios. After a signature string rake, he lowers the dynamics with organ-like double-stops beneath a tonic pedal tone. **Example 13b** features more of the same, with beautiful motivic development and an interesting blend of even and swung eighths. Play these examples fingerstyle or with hybrid picking.

Ex. 13a

Ex. 13b

Another aspect of SRV's melting-pot approach appears in **Ex. 14**, a jazzy excursion using Wes Montgomery–style octaves (play 'em with your thumb). Check out the nifty motivic development and the exceptionally cool melody played over *Am7–Em*.

Ex. 14

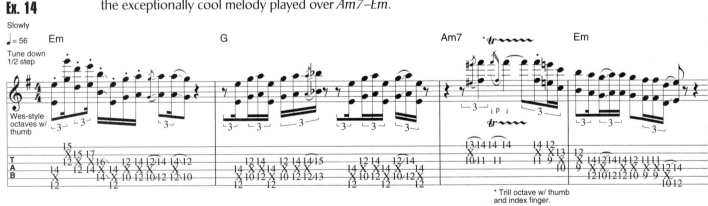

* Trill octave w/ thumb
and index finger.

Stevie Ray Vaughan once said he wanted to be known for "taking the color out of the blues." Rest in peace, bro'—it's happening.

Line Games

A Lesson with Allan Holdsworth

Originally published in Guitar Player, *February 1993.*

Allan Holdsworth's music defies description, let alone transcription. In the case of his single-note soloing, it's virtually impossible to define signature licks or phrases because Allan is a true improviser. Allan reinvents the game every time he solos.

The only way to gain insight into the Holdsworthian school of melodic line is to dissect his recorded solos. While our examples are drastically different from one another, we find recurring concepts such as legato phrasing, large interval skips (often on the same string), and motivic development. In fact, Allan's celebrated legato phrasing is often so seamless that it's difficult to tell which notes are picked. While transcribing, I frequently had to choose between several fingering possibilities. I went with what seemed most logical, but I encourage you to explore alternative fingerings.

Here, then, is a sampling of Holdsworth solo excerpts to be savored, scrutinized, and, if possible, expanded upon. And remember: As scary as these lines may seem at first, they are digested best if consumed one bite at a time.

www.GuitaRev.TrueFire.com

Example 1 illustrates Allan's sense of motific development. Over a *C* Dorian progression, he first outlines *Cmadd2* using a simple rhythm motif, and then he displaces and syncopates the figure while ascending a *B♭* major (*C* Dorian) scale on the fifth and third strings. Note how the *G* note on the fourth string is common to both motives. The third phrase (beginning at the end of bar 2) uses the eighth-position *C* pentatonic minor scale, while the fourth (bars 4 and 5) extends this idea before abruptly leaping a minor 7th. A short Dorian scale fragment targets *G*, the 5th of *Cm*.

Ex. 1

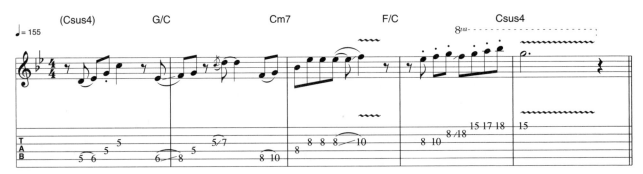

Motivic development in *Cm* is also the focus of **Ex. 2**. An ascending *C11* arpeggio targets the 9th (*D*). After a one-beat rest, the same 16th-note rhythmic motive returns, but with *E♭* as the point of arrival, producing a suspension/resolution effect. The final phrase is an extended *Cm11* arpeggio beginning with the first two notes of the original motive, but with both now played on the fifth string. This five-fret, perfect-4th stretch, a Holdsworth trademark, also occurs on the third and first strings. Practice these stretches slowly at first. Once they become comfortable, pick up the tempo and use this concept to explore new avenues out of clichédom.

Ex. 2

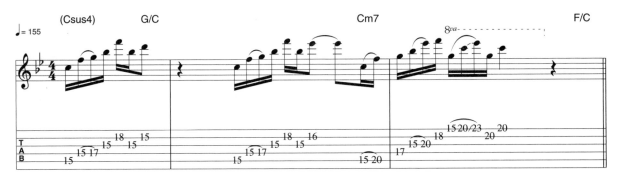

Played over a rare (for Allan!) I–IV–V progression, the short, sax-like phrase in **Ex. 3** approaches the tonic (*C*) via an arpeggiated *D♭maj7*. Next comes a five-fret pull-off, an outlined *Gsus4* (or *Csus2*), and an octave-and-a-5th pull-off from the 19th fret to the open *D* string—another favorite Holdsworth device.

Ex. 3

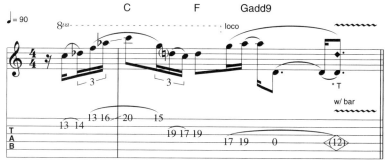

* Touch 12th fret lightly for harmonic.

Ex. 4 is a beautiful example of hammered ascending 4ths organized into a symmetrical string-skipping sequence (fifth string to third, fourth string to second, third string to first). Try this one over *Cm7*, *F7*, or *E♭maj7*.

Ex. 4

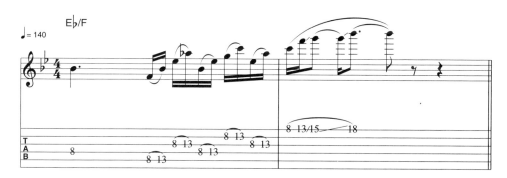

Example 5 opens with an *Ab* major (or *Db* Lydian) scale fragment, followed by a *G* major scale figure over *Gmaj13*. Note how each two-note grouping—excluding the *G* grace-note and ghosted *C*—changes strings and melodic direction. The eighth-position *Eb* major scale at the end of bar 2 anticipates the *Ab* Lydian phrases in the following measure. Allan wraps it up with a *G* pentatonic major excursion in the ninth and tenth positions.

Ex. 5

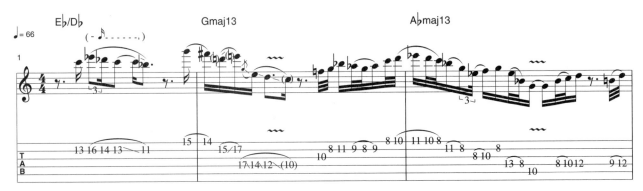

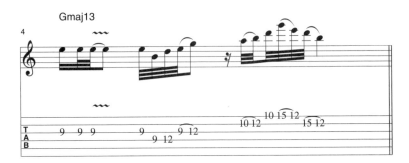

Holdsworth often travels outside the established tonality by shifting a phrase up or down a half-step. The first three notes of **Ex. 6** are derived from the thirteenth-position *F* pentatonic minor scale, while the next three shift briefly but effectively to twelfth-position *E* pentatonic minor. After a return to *F* with melodic minor and blues scale material, a descending *Bb6* (or *Gm7*) arpeggio precedes the final *C*.

Ex. 6

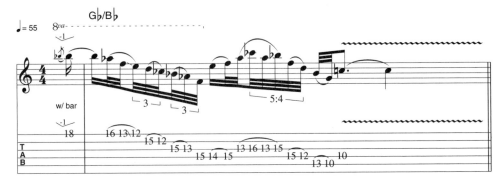

Example 7 twists and turns around *Cm7* like a world-class biker on a high-speed obstacle course. Holdsworth incorporates *C* and *Db* pentatonic-minor ideas, chromaticism, single-string melodic leaps, and *C* minor scale runs, all played legato and accelerating into the final targeted *D* note. Try playing this line over *F7* or *Ebmaj7#11*.

Ex. 7

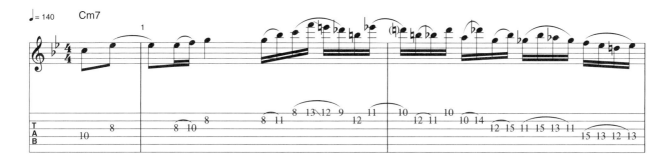

Example 8 develops a very cool perfect–4th motif. The ascending 4th is played five frets higher on the same string, and then in unison on the next highest string, the motif shifting against a primarily *Cm* background. The motif ultimately makes its way to the first and second strings, where it becomes a chromatically descending sequence. A tenth-position *C* Dorian excursion liberally sprinkled with chromatic passing tones precedes the unusually bluesy eighth-position wrap-up.

Ex. 8

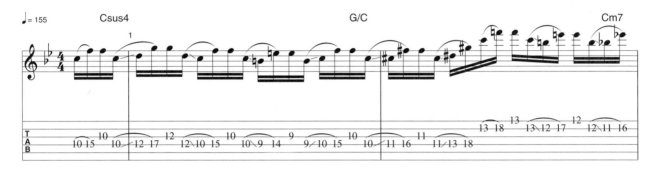

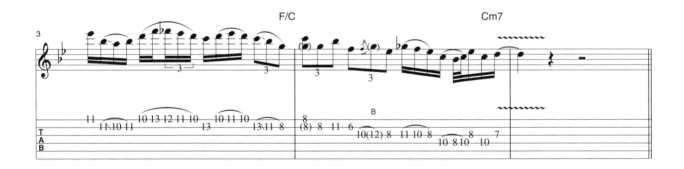

A mutated IIm–V–I–IV progression is the harmonic background to our final finger-twister (**Ex. 9**). *Bb/Gb (Gbmaj7#5)* substitutes for IIm, *Gb/Ab (Bb13b9/Ab)* subs for V, *Ebmaj7#11* is the altered I chord, and *Dsus4/Bb (Bbmaj7/6)* replaces IV. Allan starts in the seventeenth position, but by the end of the first beat he begins a series of descending half-step position shifts to accommodate the line's increasing chromaticism. Reaching the eleventh position at the end of beat *three*, he reverses direction, ascending to the fifteenth position for the *Gb/Ab*. Here Allan employs a fragment of a symmetrical G diminished scale (half-step, whole-step, etc.). The phrase culminates in an unexpected slide to the 21st fret and some melodic tremolo-bar scooping (another Holdsworth hallmark). Working his way into the eighth position via an *Eb* major scale, Allan superimposes a stretchy *Fsus4* arpeggio before continuing to develop a descending motif derived from *Eb* major. Bar 4 features a stripped-down pentatonic approach to an ascending octave skip, a half-step descent, and a pull-off to the open E string.

Ex. 9

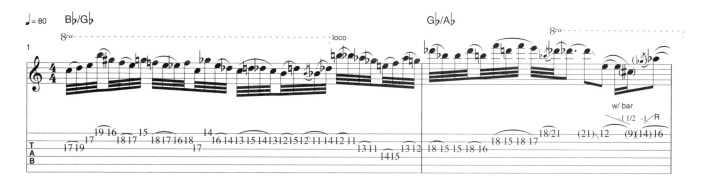

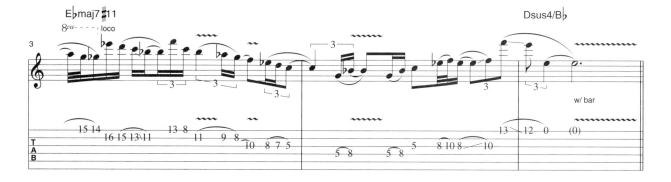

Solo Transcription

John McLaughlin

"Birds of Fire"

Originally published in Guitar Player, *November 2000.*

There has likely never been another five-piece instrumental ensemble as powerfully virtuosic, creative, and downright *scary* as the original Mahavishnu Orchestra. You'd be hard-pressed to name a band that shook the world the way Mahavishnu did from 1971 to '73. Though the Orchestra's music wasn't aimed at the masses, their strange and beautiful sound opened a lot of ears and reached a wide audience. And for young musicians, the blend of classical composition, jazz improvisation, Eastern melodies, and screaming Marshalls proved irresistible. In its short, three-album existence, the Mahavishnu Orchestra pushed the boundaries of compositional and improvisational interplay and paved the way for fusion groups to follow.

Formed by guitarist extraordinaire John McLaughlin, the front line also included Prague-born keyboardist Jan Hammer (whose self-styled "country and eastern" approach defined the Orchestra's sound as much as McLaughlin's guitar) and Jerry Goodman, a classically trained violinist who was a founding member of Chicago prog-rockers the Flock. Anchoring the band were the powerhouse drummer Billy Cobham and bassist Rick Laird. In concert, the band dazzled audiences with rapid-fire improvisations and impromptu guitar/drum duets, but this flashiness was rooted in compositions as deep as the ocean.

McLaughlin's musical vision evolved fairly rapidly and can be easily traced. The pot began simmering with his work on Miles Davis's *Jack Johnson* and *Bitches Brew,* came to a boil with Tony Williams' *Emergency!* and McLaughlin's own *Extrapolation* and *Devotion,* and blew its lid with Mahavishnu's *The Inner Mounting Flame, Birds of Fire,* and *Between Nothingness and Eternity*—three albums that simply must be heard to be believed.

To understand McLaughlin's "Birds of Fire" solo, we must first investigate the music behind it. **Example 1** shows a mini-score reduction of the harmonic and rhythmic layers that support the song's melody and high-octane soloing.

The song begins a brisk eighth-note = 384 BPM tempo, but soon the exuberant band accelerates to 412 BPM! McLaughlin's spooky, phase-shifted electric 12-string arpeggios, played on a double-neck

Gibson SG, sound like a harpsichord. Hammer doubles these arpeggios on a Fender Rhodes to create a two-bar figure identical to the one that penetrates the song's opening gong-punctuated silent meditation. McLaughlin's ingenious voicings essentially consist of two dominant-7th chords played a whole-step apart (A♭7 and B♭7) against open-B and open-E pedal tones. These open strings function as the #5 (E) and #9 (B) of A♭7, and the enharmonic ♭5 (F♭) and ♭9 (C♭) of B♭7. McLaughlin uses all four altered tones over the course of both chords. This keeps the tension factor high.

The 18/8 meter breaks into three different metric sub-groupings, depending on the instrument:

- The guitar and electric piano use an eighth-note pulse divided into three groups of 5/8 and one of 3/8. You could use alternate picking for the entire figure, but I recommend the notated hybrid picking.
- The electric violin (played pizzicato) and bass parts are based on a half-timed 9/4 pulse grouped 4/4–3/4–2/4 or 4/4–5/4. This is the easiest groove to follow.
- To ice the cake, Cobham plays a 6/8 double-kick groove three times per measure, and anticipates a surprise crash cymbal on the 18th eighth-note. This throws the entire figure off kilter, except when Cobham occasionally nails the *one*. Begin very slowly (around 120 BPM), increase the tempo gradually, and you'll soon experience the thrill of locking into any of these parts with confidence.

Ex. 1

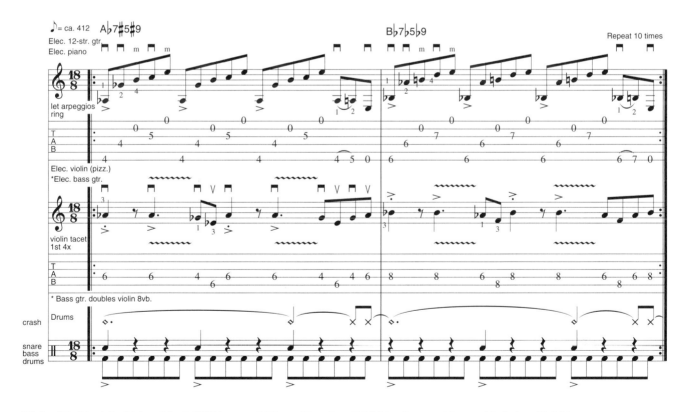

"Birds of Fire" by John McLaughlin © 1973 (renewed) Warner-Tamerlane Publishing Corp. and Basque Music, Inc. All rights administered by Warner-Tamerlane Publishing Corp. All rights reserved. Used by permission.

Let's switch necks and tackle McLaughlin's 6-string solo (**Ex. 2**). In his superb, self-penned *John McLaughlin and the Mahavishnu Orchestra* songbook [Warner Bros., out of print], the guitarist suggests using synthetic *A♭* and *B♭* super-Locrian modes (root, ♭2, ♭3, 3, ♭5, ♭6, ♭7) over the *A♭7* to *B♭7* progression. But instead of following his own advice, McLaughlin heaps on gobs of *E* pentatonic minor for the majority of his 20-bar excursion. Even though it's in the "wrong" key, this scale produces many of the altered tones found in both chords, and it actually grounds the progression by creating a sense of familiarity. To get a handle on McLaughlin's rhythms, break each measure into three bars of 6/8 or 3/4.

McLaughlin begins his blowing with what appears to be three bars of fifth-position *A* pentatonic minor "blues box" phrases, but closer inspection reveals that he's emphasizing the 4th of *E* pentatonic minor. In bar 2 he accents the second eighth-note in each 6/8 subgroup. The last phrase in bar 3 confirms the *E* minor pentatonic tonality, and initiates an ascending series of four-note motifs (bars 4 and 5) that include a Dorian-inducing *F♯* (the 2nd, or 9th). The first of McLaughlin's many screeching overbends appear in bar 6. (Yes, that's a *C♮*. It functions as 3rd of *A♭7* and 9th of *B♭7*.) He nails every eighth-note in bar 7 before beginning a bar-and-a-half descent to low *E*. Check out those sliding, *G*-string position shifts.

As McLaughlin blazes into bars 9 and 10, his rhythms become a bit blurry. You can hear him lock into a two-against-three feel a third of the way through bar 11, immediately preceding the Martian blues run in bar 12. Bar 13 reprises both the *C* overbends and superimposed two-against-three feel, and bar 15 sets up a string of ascending 5/8 motifs that extend through bar 16. Starting at bar 17, McLaughlin touches on and then settles into two final measures of two-against-three accented overbends.

Ex. 2

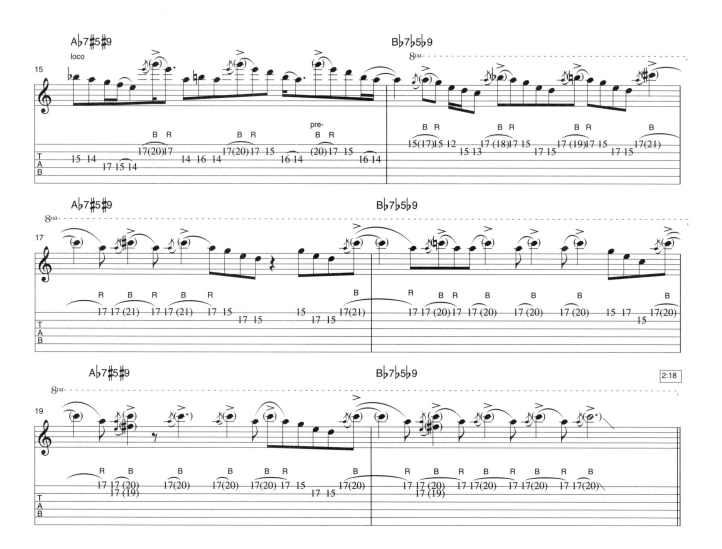

Throughout his solo, you'll hear McLaughlin phrase eighth-notes in groups of 3, 4, 5, and 6, but why stop there? To develop your ability to solo in 18/8, practice *all* subgroupings. Here's a breakdown of eighth-note subgroups in a measure of 18/8:

- 9 x 2/8
- 6 x 3/8
- 4 x 4/8 + 2/8
- 3 x 5/8 + 3/8
- 3 x 6/8
- 2 x 7/8 + 4/8
- 2 x 8/8 + 2/8
- 2 x 9/8

Once you've got a grip on these subgroups, try mixing them up. For instance: 5/8 + 4/8 + 4/8 + 5/8, or 4/8 + 3/8 + 2/8 + 4/8 + 3/8 + 2/8, and so on. Goodness gracious, great birds o' fire!

Style Lesson
Passion & Fretwear
An Aural History of the Vai Decade, 1983–1993

Originally published in Guitar Player, *September 1993.*

Having demonstrated a sophisticated grasp of music theory and uncanny technical command of his instrument for over a decade, Steve Vai stands at the pinnacle of his art. Years of hard work and focused study spawned a style that is widely emulated, but Vai remains one of those rare visionaries who plays from the head, hands, *and* heart.

The Oct. '84 issue of *Guitar Player*, with its recording of Vai's "The Attitude Song" (from *Flex-Able*) and Steve's transcription, triggered an epidemic of beaded foreheads and increased pulse rates as players scrambled back to the woodshed. ("Can anyone really play like that? He actually puts the *B* string under his fingernail and bends it around the back of the neck!") You could hear 'em for miles.

Many were first exposed to Steve's playing through his recordings with Alcatrazz, David Lee Roth, or Whitesnake. But remember, Vai was Frank Zappa's "stunt guitarist" while still in his teens. Steve honed his already ample ensemble and solo chops on Frank's fiendishly difficult "impossible guitar parts," which became even more complex during Vai's tenure. Check out Zappa's *Tinseltown Rebellion, You Are What You Is, Ship Arriving Too Late To Save a Drowning Witch, The Man from Utopia, Them or Us*, and volumes 1, 3, 4, 5, and 6 of the live series *You Can't Do That on Stage Anymore*. You'll experience some of the most incredible musical performances ever.

With a degree from the School of Zappa, Vai went on to become one of rock's MVPs, and licks like **Ex. 1a** help explain why. The astonishing pinched artificial harmonics are produced from the same fretted position while the pick hand goes fishin'. Begin by locating the *E* harmonic two octaves and a 5th above the fretted fundamental *A*. On a typical Strat, this node should fall in the center pickup region (theoretically speaking, where the 33rd fret would be). Bend up

FREE Audio Version Online
www.GuitaRev.TrueFire.com

a whole-step for the *F#* harmonic, and then hold the bend and move your pick attack slightly closer to the bridge for the *A*. Remain in that spot and release the bend to cover the *G♮*. The trick is to simultaneously shift your picking hand while bending or releasing for the following *F#*'s and *G*'s. Remember, only the harmonics should be audible. The artificial harmonics in **Ex. 1b** are all pinched one octave above their fretted positions. Learn the shape of the melody (basically, a descending *A9* arpeggio) without harmonics, and then pinch the same shape 12 hypothetical frets higher.

Ex. 1a

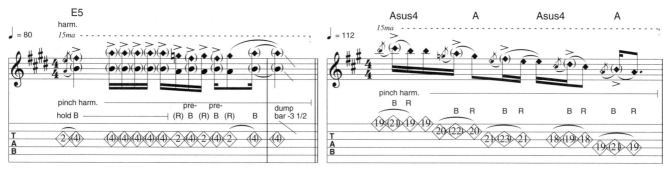

In Vai's hands, the whammy bar is no mere effect, but a controlled tool of expression. He was the first person I ever heard play melodies by hitting a single note and maneuvering the bar to other discrete pitches. **Example 2** shows one melodic possibility inherent in a single natural harmonic. Your bar must be set to raise the *G* string at least a major 3rd (two whole-steps) to pull this one off properly.

Clean, arpeggiated natural harmonics chime over fretted bass notes in **Examples 3a** and **3b**. Pay close attention to the tricky fingering in order to properly align the 1st and 4th fingers in position to play the harmonics. A bit of chorus and compression will help bring out the chime.

Ex. 2   **Ex. 3a**

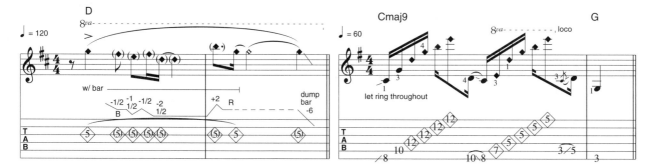

Ex. 3b

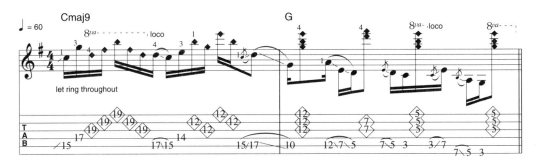

Vai's chord-melody stylings are deeply rooted in Hendrix. Unexpected open strings pop up in the middle of **Ex. 4**'s pretty "Little Wing"–style embellishments. The votes on the official name for the technique shown in **Ex. 5** haven't been tallied yet, but contenders include "flutter," "warble," and "purr." Regardless, Steve found a way to make musical use of what most players considered an annoying side effect of locking tremolos. Here, you articulate notes by picking the bar and letting it spring back abruptly after each attack.

Ex. 4

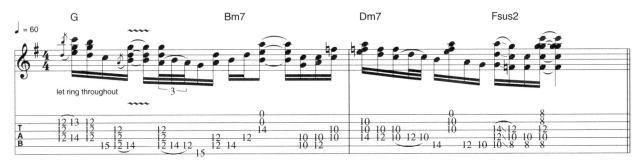

Ex. 5

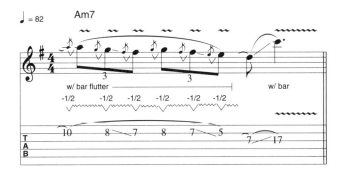

Steve's "talking guitar" is legendary. When conversing in this manner, he'll often use a wah-wah pedal for more vowel-like articulations, as in **Ex. 6**. The short, descending *D* minor phrase in **Ex. 7** shifts from 17th to 12th position via a six-note motif. The outlined *Dm7* is followed by *Gm7* and a repeat of the *Dm7* motif an octave lower.

Ex. 6

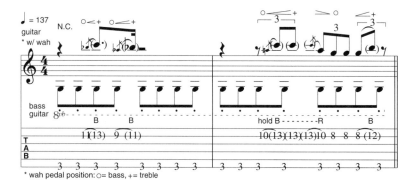

* wah pedal position: ○= bass, += treble

Ex. 7

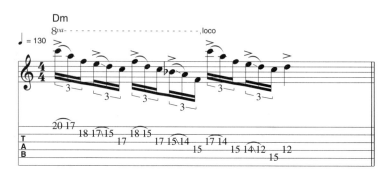

The *D* Dorian-based octaves and 5hs in **Ex. 8a** are typical of Steve's smooth use of wide-interval skips. **Example 8b** finds two melodies converging from opposite directions until they meet in the middle. The *F* harmonic background creates a Lydian tonality, one of Vai's favorites.

Ex. 8a   Ex. 8b

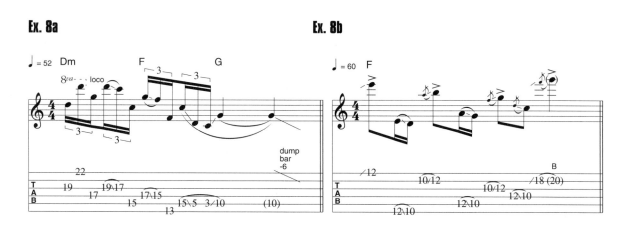

Steve has also taken two-hand tapping to new heights. The tapped high-*F#* pedal in **Ex. 9a** triggers pull-offs to a moving *E* major line played entirely on the *B* string before concluding with a short legato run. The *A* and *B* background chords imply a shifting Lydian/Mixolydian climate. For the first three measures of devilishly fast tapping in **Ex. 9b**, keep in mind that you are simply sequencing a descending *A* minor scale motif entirely on the *G* string. The symmetrical quintuplets in the fourth bar switch the emphasis to *A* pentatonic minor. The repeating figure in **Ex. 9c** sounds great alone but really comes to life when played through a delay set for a single eighth-note repeat at the same volume as the original signal.

Ex. 9a

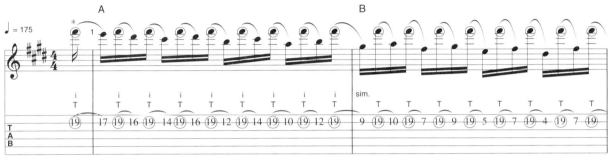

* ○ = Tap w/ indicated pick hand finger.
i – index, m = middle

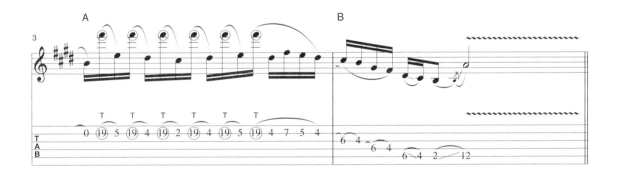

Ex. 9b

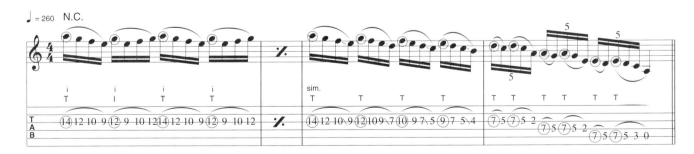

Ex. 9c

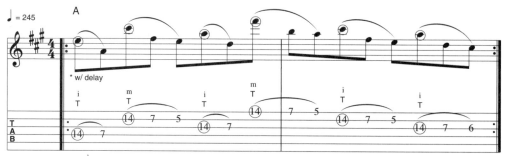

* Delay set for single ♪ repeat.
Delay mix = 50/50.

The sequenced legato run in **Ex. 10a** is conceptually similar to the tapped sequence in Ex. 9b. One pick attack starts the ball rolling. **Example 10b** contrasts sweep-picking with legato phrasing in *D* Dorian. The swept grace-notes ascend in 4ths while the target notes spell out a descending *Am7* arpeggio. Steve concludes with a silky descending run.

Ex. 10a

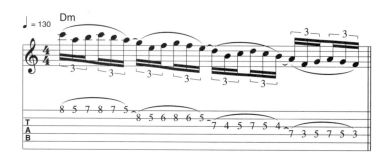

Ex. 10b

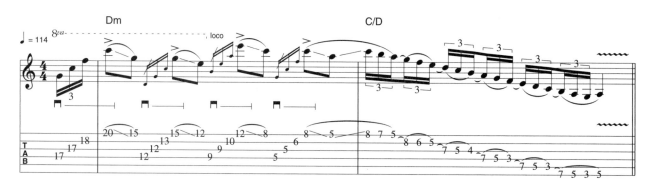

The ascending diatonic scale sequence in **Ex. 11a** takes advantage of an open-*E* pedal and up-beat eighth-note position changes. Note how it could easily be extended in the opposite direction. Another Lydian-flavored diatonic sequence in the first half of **Ex. 11b** intersperses arpeggiated *E, D, C#m, Bm,* and *A* triads with an open-*E* pedal point prior to another striking legato run.

Ex. 11a

Ex. 11b

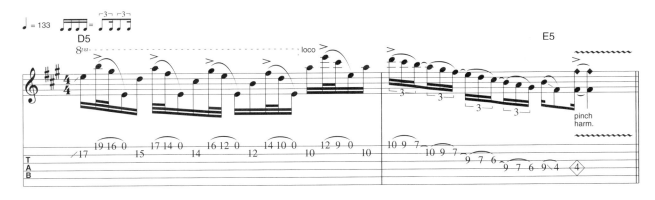

The sequenced melodic motif in **Ex. 12** has been harmonized in first-inversion triads to further enhance the *F* Lydian tonality. All the notes are diatonically related to the parent key of *C* major. Remember, any scale fragment or motif may be given the same treatment. The Lydian melody in the bottom part of **Ex. 13** has resurfaced several times throughout Vai's career. This version adds a fourth voice to the triadic harmony, producing some very close intervals (minor and major 2nds). The results almost make you feel like you're sitting in a pool of warm water.

Ex. 12

Ex. 13

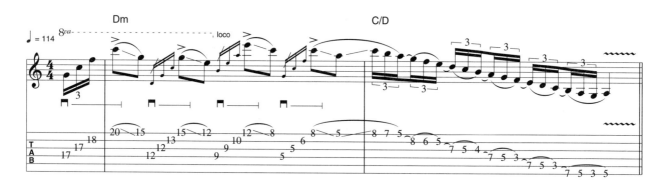

The legato excursion in **Ex. 14** is downright scary! Beginning with a single attack, glide seamlessly across strings using only bends, hammers, pull-offs, slides, and bar articulations for a whopping measure and a half. The ascending and descending sweeps beginning midway through the second bar outline *Em*, *Dm*, and *Am* triads. The run climaxes with a textbook example of the infamous "I'm squirting now" bend. (Just a joke, folks—check out *The Real Frank Zappa Book* [Fireside] for an explanation.)

Ex. 13

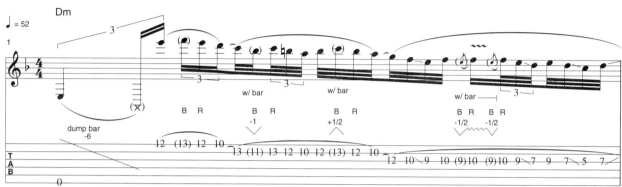

Exploring the Crystal Planet

An Exclusive Lesson with Joe Satriani

Originally published in Guitar Player, *May 1998.*

After releasing several tracked-live-in-the-studio albums and touring with G3, Joe Satriani can no longer keep his experimental side in check. *Crystal Planet* delivers the hardest-hitting batch of instrumentals since his landmark '87 release, *Surfing with the Alien*. Though his soloing is as heartfelt and stunning as ever, it's Satch's composing abilities that take centerstage.

We met Satriani in San Francisco for an inside look at six tunes from the new record. Seated at a large antique table in Bill Graham's former office and cradling his chrome Ibanez, Satriani revealed psycho-acoustic secrets, offered insights into his composing techniques, and provided a guided tour of his fretboard. Here are highlights from our inspiring encounter.

"One concept for the album was to have a sequence of songs in ascending keys," says Satriani. "I'm very excited that I was able to make this happen. You know how certain recordings are really great, but you can't listen to them from top to bottom? I thought, 'Why not make an album that is uplifting from one song to the next?' I took this to heart when I compiled the tunes."

Satriani was equally determined to keep his guitar tracks spontaneous and fun. "I wanted to just pick up my guitar and play my parts. I didn't want the music to be too brooding." Instead of anguishing over every detail in his solos, Satriani opted to step back and look at the big picture. "It's all about arranging. Sometimes you'll have to record a tune ten different ways before you stumble on the idea that makes the whole thing work. Form is more important than the soloist's ego. In the end, you get a more listenable record with greater longevity."

Strains of electronica permeate *Crystal Planet*. "I wanted three musicians playing live in the studio," Satriani explains, "but I also wanted to embrace technology. We had the option to record live as well as slowly layer tracks from the ground up. Sometimes we used the computer to stimulate us musically. For example, 'Crystal Planet' and 'With Jupiter in Mind' are live performances, but first we hired Eric Caudieux to create electronica versions of the songs to put us in the mood. As a trio, we played to the computer as if it was a fourth member, just driving us like crazy. That affected our performances. It made me step on my Fulltone Ultimate Octave pedal and choose those really weird notes in the solo. When we mixed, we didn't use all 58 tracks of gurgling, throbbing electronica—we just picked one or two. Jamming to the computer helped us finish the record in six weeks."

"Up in the Sky," the album's opening tune, explodes with a flurry of sequencer-like harmonics over a pumping *E* bass. "Like Prodigy meets Van Halen!" laughs Satriani. "I hadn't thought about how to pick it until we started to record. I came up with this [**Ex. 1a**]. It's one of several songs on the album that are based on Native American music. I wanted to keep the theme of going up. I eventually played the melody on the bottom strings at the 10th and 12th frets [**Ex. 1b**], even though it took some EQ reduction to make it less tubby. Mike Fraser—the producer—decided he liked the grittiness."

Ex. 1a

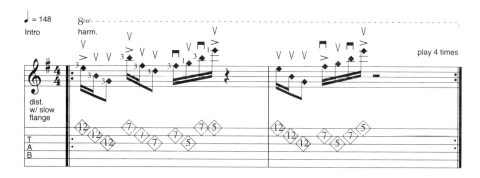

Ex. 1b

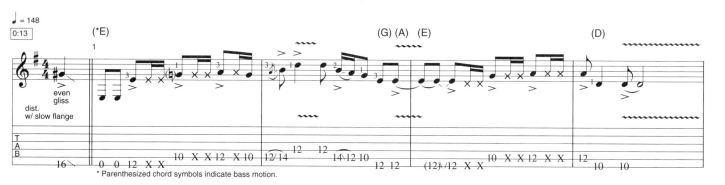

* Parenthesized chord symbols indicate bass motion.

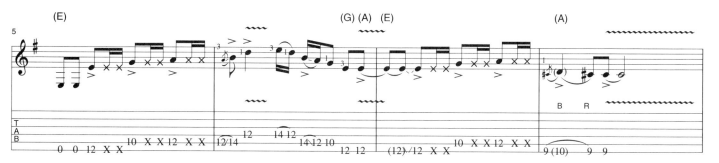

"Up in the Sky" by Joe Satriani © 1998 Strange Beautiful Music (ASCAP). International copyright secured. All rights reserved.

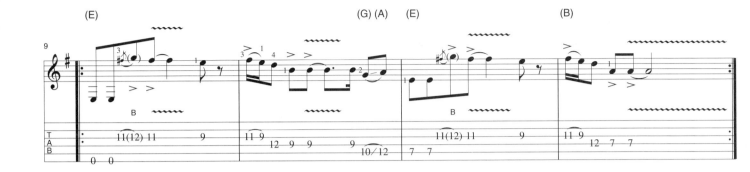

The intro to "Crystal Planet" (**Ex. 2a**) derives an exotic flavor from the key of *B* minor. "That's an energy part," says Satriani. "Now my computer makes that sound when it starts up. I made a little .WAV file and stuck it in there." At 0:27, he revisits this part and gives it a new twist (**Ex. 2b**). "That's part of the 'make it fun' routine. It goes from this Arabic-sounding riff to a pretty, lyrical *B* minor melody."

Ex. 2a

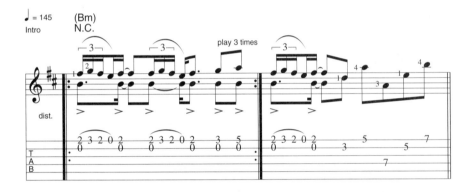

Ex. 2b

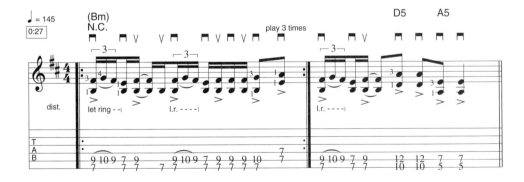

"Crystal Planet" by Joe Satriani © 1998 Strange Beautiful Music (ASCAP). International copyright secured. All rights reserved.

The bridge theme (**Ex. 2c**) features a nifty ascending #4–5–9 motif. "The bridge gets you a half-step away from the return of the chorus. For me, wow, that's dramatic! The rhythm part was originally this [*plays busy syncopated 16th-note strums similar to the rhythm of Ex. 2b, using Ex. 2c's chords*], but it never made the record." Instead, Satriani arpeggiated the voicings on a guitar synth, gating its grand-piano patch with a track of electronic percussion.

"The solo starts in *E*," says Satriani while playing **Ex. 2d**. "All the fretted notes are left-hand hammers. At the end of the song, I move to the first and second strings [**Ex. 2e**]."

Ex. 2c

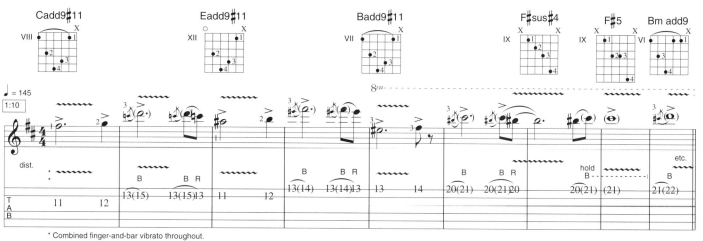

* Combined finger-and-bar vibrato throughout.

Ex. 2d

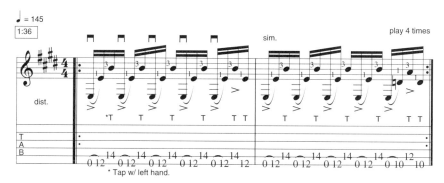

* Tap w/ left hand.

Ex. 2e

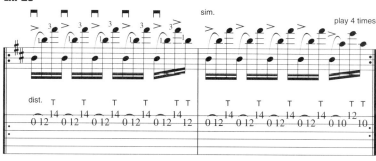

In "Trundrumbalind," Satriani establishes a recurring two-bar 5/4 rhythm motif at the outset (**Ex. 3a**). "This fingering keeps things quiet. The third time around, I add the second string on beat *four*. You can barely hear it because the guitar tone is kind of woolly, but I'm hearing that melody in my head as I'm playing." At 3:49, the level drops for a spooky whole-tone interlude (**Ex. 3b**). "It's basically two fingerings that move around. It goes *A7, G, F7* [written enharmonically as *E#7*], *C#*, and then *A7, G, D#7*, and *B*."

Like the calm before the storm, Ex. 3b sets the stage for an explosive outro. "One of my favorite moments on the record is that ending section. It's so out, and Jeff Campitelli comes in with the weirdest drum thing, and then Stu Hamm adds a McCartney-like ascending bass line."

Ex. 3a

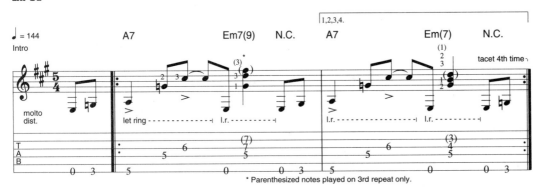

Ex. 3b

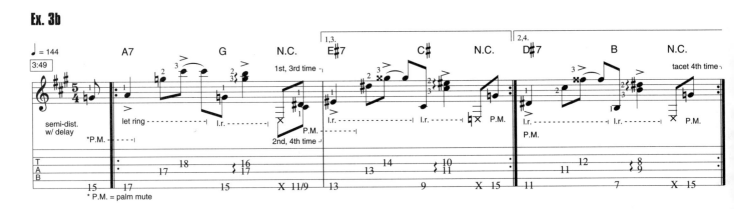

"Trundrumbalind" by Joe Satriani © 1998 Strange Beautiful Music (ASCAP). International copyright secured. All rights reserved.

My interpretation of the "Raspberry Jam Delta-V" intro (**Ex. 4a**) elicited a hearty chuckle from Satriani. "That's the version you use when you're in front of people who hate when guitar players show off. I figured out a similar way to play it so people would think, 'Oh, he's not trying to show off.' In fact, the way I originally wrote it is a shameless display of technique that would have been very popular ten years ago. It requires reaching over with your right hand and fretting two B's on the third and first strings, while letting the open-B string ring [**Ex. 4b**]. Then, with your left hand, tap the melody notes on the top three strings between the 9th and 12th frets [**Ex. 4c**]. See, there's always a B ready underneath." *Psst*: The octave jump in the fourth ending is courtesy of Satriani's red DigiTech Whammy pedal.

How will he play this passage live? "You know what? I'm gonna trip out, depending on who's in the audience," he laughs.

Ex. 4a

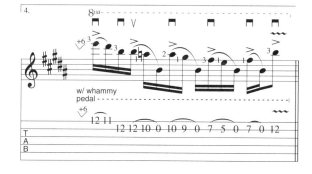

Ex. 4b

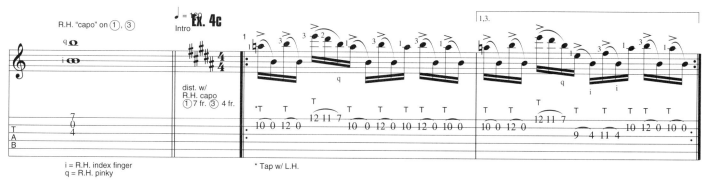

"Raspberry Jam Delta-V" by Joe Satriani © 1998 Strange Beautiful Music (ASCAP). International copyright secured. All rights reserved.

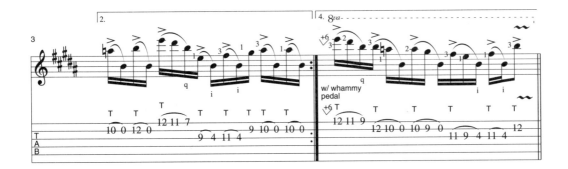

In the intro to the epic "With Jupiter in Mind," four ascending chord voicings create shifting tonalities on an *E* pitch axis (**Ex. 5a**). "It's Dorian/Lydian, Dorian/Lydian," Satriani explains. An ingenious bass riff (**Ex. 5b**) defines the changes by emphasizing the ♭7, 4, and ♭3, then the 7, ♯4, and 3. "I played it on one string using a '58 Telecaster," he says.

Ex. 5a

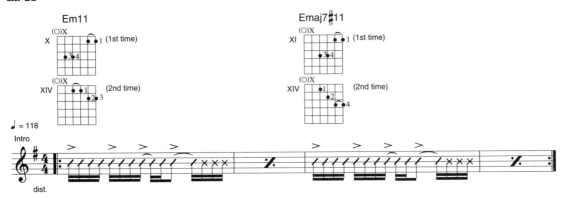

Ex. 5b

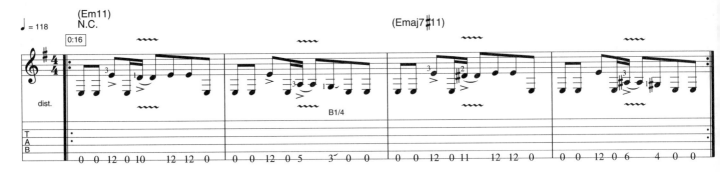

"With Jupiter in Mind" by Joe Satriani © 1998 Strange Beautiful Music (ASCAP). International copyright secured. All rights reserved.

Ex. 5c, the first half of the song's melody and rhythm figure, melds bluesy calls with an unusual bent major 7th over Ex. 5b's shifting *E* Dorian/Lydian pad. Check out those ascending arpeggios in the rhythm part.

Ex. 5c

From this point, things get quite playful. "It's almost a theme-and-variations thing. I borrow the rhythm and contour from the chorus melody [**Ex. 5d**], and transpose the line from *E* Dorian and *E* Lydian to *A* Hungarian major [**Ex. 5e**]. Finally, after all these years, I found a use for this scale! It's like a symmetrical [half/whole diminished] scale without a ♭2. I solo back and forth between *E* and *A* Hungarian major, and when I finally get back to the tune, it's like my wormhole idea: 'Wow! Where have you been, and how did I get back to the beginning of the song again?'"

Ex. 5d

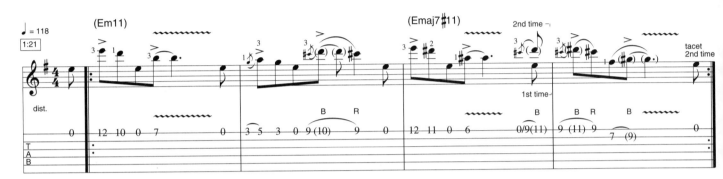

Ex. 5e

Crystal Planet ends with "Z.Z.'s Song." "It was a live performance at Fantasy Studios. I had my amp cranked, so I used this fingering [**Ex. 6**] to keep everything quiet except the notes I wanted to sound. Sometimes fingerings that seem logical in your living room aren't practical at loud levels."

Special thanks to Kevin Burns and BGP.

Ex. 6

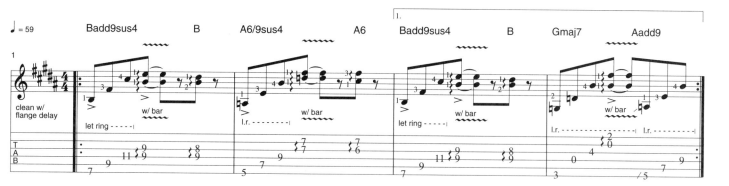

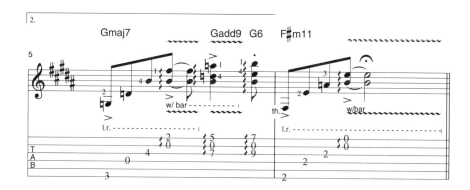

"Z.Z.'s Song" by Joe Satriani © 1998 Strange Beautiful Music (ASCAP). International copyright secured. All rights reserved.

Danny Gatton

"Harlem Nocturne"

Originally published in Guitar Player, *July 1993.*

Danny Gatton's incredible rendition of Earl Hagen and Dick Rogers' "Harlem Nocturne" had been a live show-stopper for years. The fireworks were finally captured on *Cruisin' Deuces*, in which Danny burns through the four-bar intro, 16-bar melody, and 10-bar bridge sections with deceptive ease, unleashing just about every technique known to guitarkind with style, grace, and a sizzling, reverb-enhanced Teletone that won't quit. While the recording features a rhythm guitar and several overdubs, this transcription has been arranged for one guitar. I haven't indicated every detail of Danny's right-hand pick-and-fingers technique, since the pages already resemble swarms of flies.

The slinky intro figure slips seamlessly into the melody, conjuring images of pulp-magazine private eyes by emphasizing the wicked-sounding major 7th over the tonic E minor. Similar tension arises from the A♭ melody note over the D9♭5 chord. Note Danny's impeccable phrasing of the melody throughout the A sections (in particular, check out the pickup to the melody in bars 12 and 13). Gatton's distinctive pinched artificial harmonics (he strikes the string with the pick held between his thumb and index finger while simultaneously plucking upwards *behind* the pick with his middle finger) segue to a volume-swelled major-3rd bend (!) that gradually releases to the major 7th. Too cool! And listen closely to how the first two harmonics move in contrary motion to the melody—supernatural stuff, folks.

Gatton resorts to Lenny Breau–style artificial harmonics for the *Amadd9* arpeggio in bar 14. The chromatic run in bar 20 leads into the bridge section (B) in the relative major key of G. After some sliding, Memphis-style 6th/9th chording, Danny's trademark "Orange Blossom Special" tone-knob wah shows up in bars 22 and 23. Gatton maintains fever-pitch intensity with two exceptions: the jazzy chord-melody breakdowns in bars 27–28 and 53–54. In order to name the chords, I've labeled the root motion as a series of back-cycled IIm–V progressions descending in whole-steps and converging on *B7#9/♭9*, tonic *E* minor's altered dominant.

Danny kicks off the solo section (C1) with bluesy pickin' that develops a stutter on a gradually released bend in bar 33. He gets a convincing Bigsby effect using neck vibrato in bar 36. The pedal-point motif developed over bars 39 and 40 maintains a classical flavor without sacrificing the James Bond vibe. (The stretchy fingerings appear in **Figure 1**.) Chord-melody fragments in bars 41 and 42 give way to a stellar bending excursion from a single fretted position in bars 43 and 44.

Fig. 1

The bridge solo (D) begins with slippery, country-style double- and triple-stops, then gets bluesier over the IV chord (C6) in bars 51 and 52. The restated chordal breakdown adds a low voice to each m7#5 voicing and confirms the descending IIm–V root movement. A very cool chordal superimposition, *A13* over *Em*, is arpeggiated as a fractured quintuplet, winding down the solo and allowing a bit of breathing space before the melodic onslaught at letter E. Danny gets off a good "whistler" before reaching behind the nut to bend the open-*G* string in bar 59. The dramatic ascending chordal figure in bar 63 ushers in the wild and crazy free-time ending cadenza, the most subjective part of this transcription by far.

Gatton's every phrase deserves special attention, but after you've learned and incorporated them, take the ultimate lesson from this Tele master: Never play it the same way twice.

Harlem Nocturne

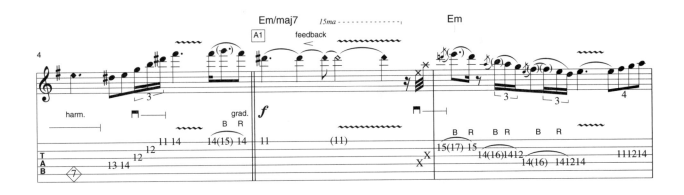

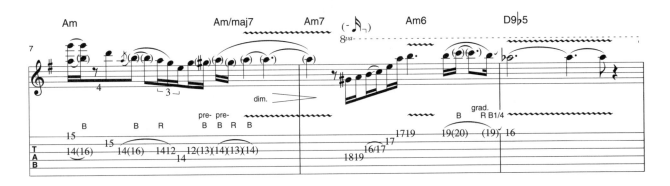

"Harlem Nocturne" music by Earle Hagen © 1940, 1946, 1951 Shapiro, Bernstein & Co., Inc., New York. Copyright renewed. International copyright secured. All rights reserved. Used by permission.

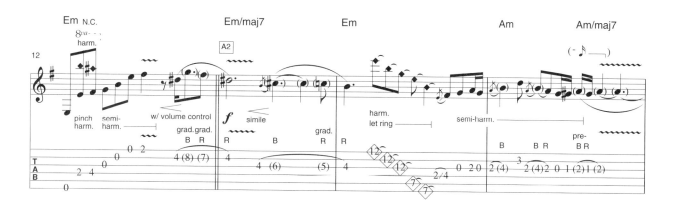

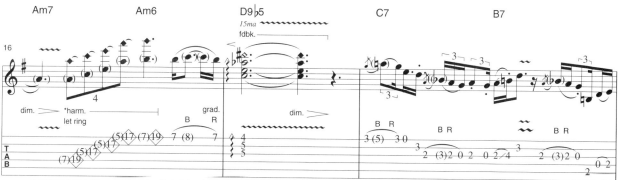

* Artificial harmonics — touch node with right-hand index finger.

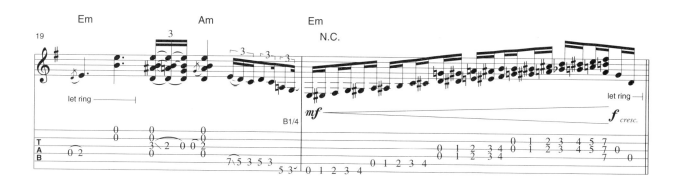

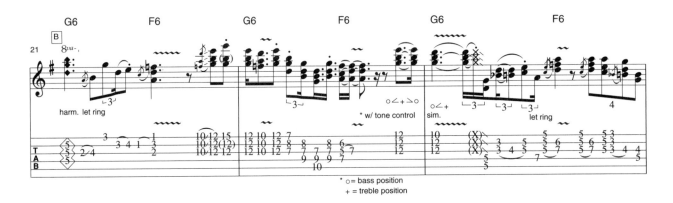

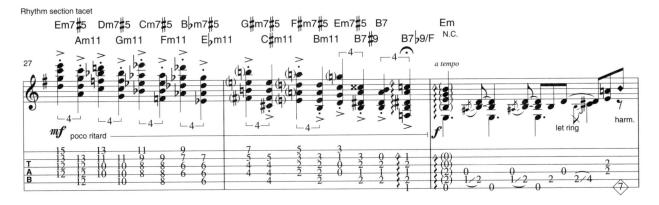

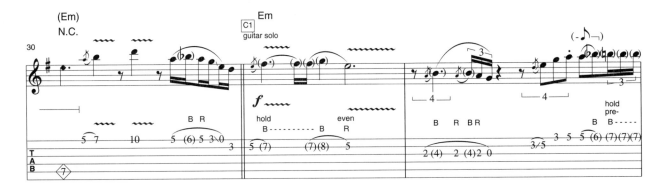

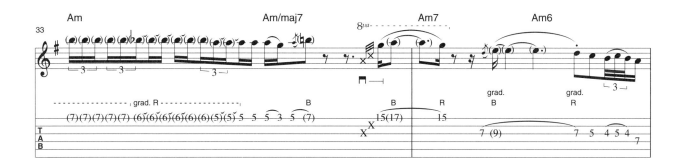

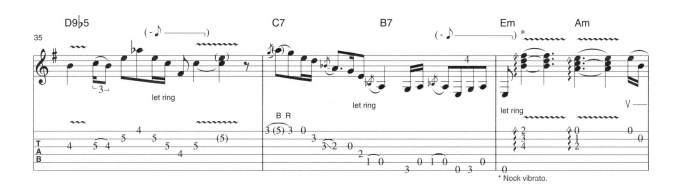

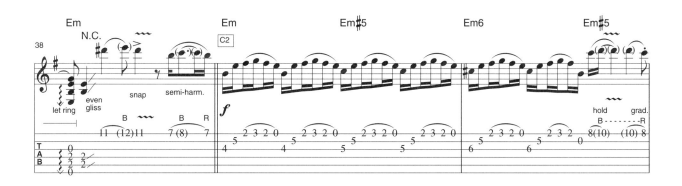

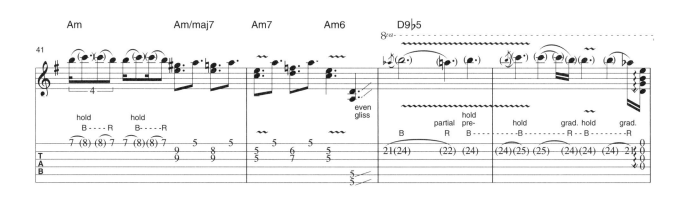

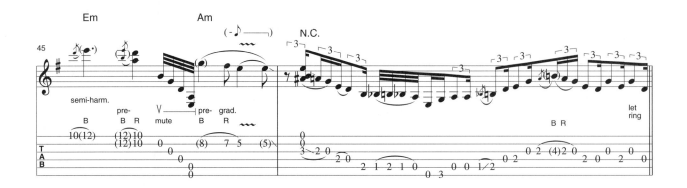

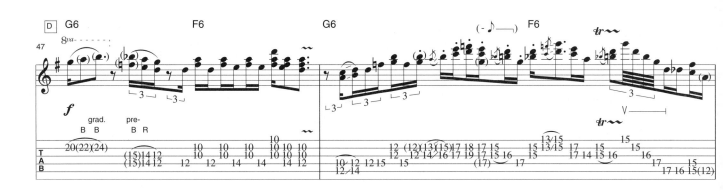

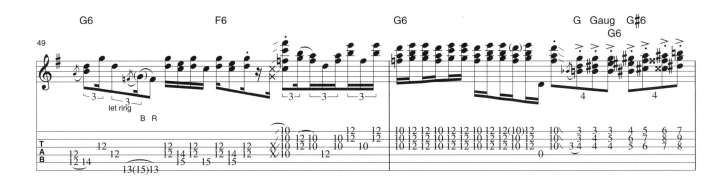

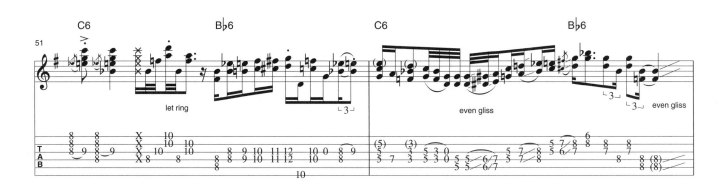

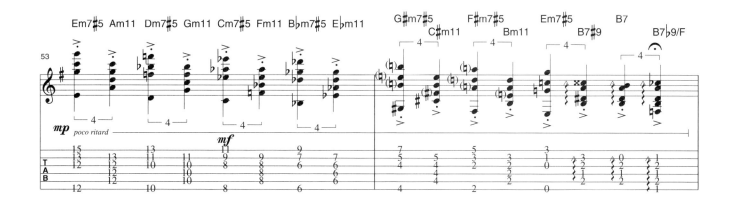

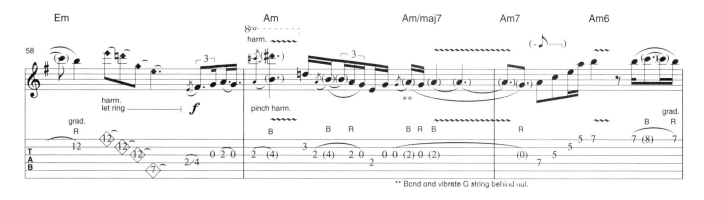

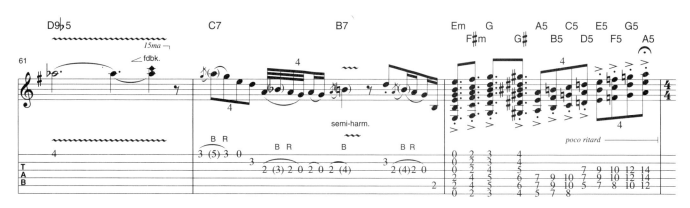

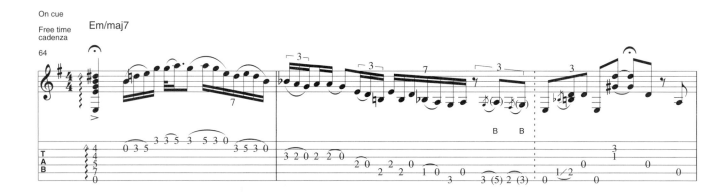

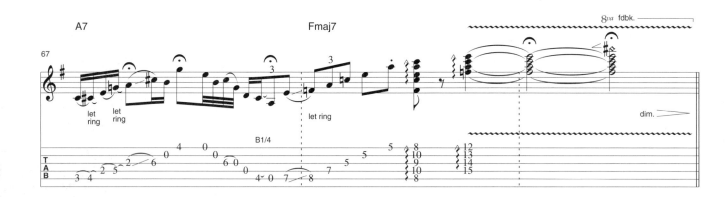

Mike Stern

Monster II–V–I's

Originally published in Guitar Player, *July 1993.*

The IIm–V–I is the most common progression in jazz, but that doesn't stop Mike Stern from putting his own stamp on these ubiquitous changes, as demonstrated by these examples drawn from his improvisations. While bopping his way with easy confidence through treacherous IIm–V–I modulations, Mike often draws from his expansive rock/blues vocabulary—a nearly heretical approach to jazz standards.

Example 1 features straight-ahead bop blowing over a IIm–V–I in B♭. The pickup into the first measure approaches the 5th of the IIm chord (*Cm7*) via two descending chromatic tones. The rhythmic motif reappears, leading to the 5th of the V chord (*F7*) and setting the listener up for the return to the I chord (*B♭maj7*). Instead, Stern sustains the V chord, sliding into the twelfth position and stirring up melodic tension with a series of descending chromatic pull-offs. Grab the *F* on beat *three* with your 3rd finger to shift into eleventh position for the *B♭* major wrap-up.

Ex. 1

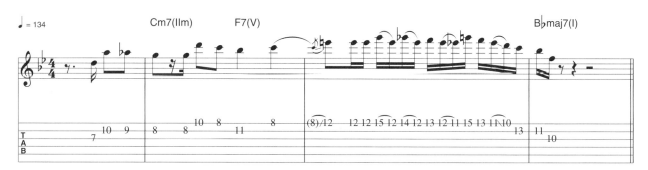

The line in **Ex. 2** was originally conceived over a C minor IIm–V–Im (*Dm7♭5-G7-Cm*), but it works just as well over its relative major progression (*Fm7–B♭7–E♭maj7*). The motif in beats *one* and *two* derives from *A♭* Dorian, an "outside" tonality produced by raising the IIm chord–*Fm7*, in the case of the major progression–a minor 3rd to *A♭m* (which is also a ♭5 substitute for *Dm7♭5*, the IIm of the minor progression). The remainder of the line utilizes the *E♭* major scale to create altered-chord dissonances (♯5, ♭5, ♭9) over the *G7* chord. Note that only diatonic dissonances (♭7, 9, 11) occur when the phrase is played against *B♭7*.

Ex. 2

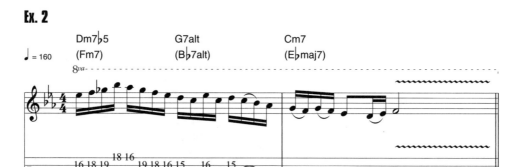

In **Ex. 3**, the third of the tonic *B♭* is approached by a short altered dominant 7♯9/♭9 lick. We can also view these notes as part of the *E♭* minor scale, which demonstrates a handy chord substitution technique: To create altered tension over a dominant seventh chord, play from the minor chord situated a whole-step below the dominant chord. Next, Stern unleashes a series of King-style blues phrases (complete with B.B.'s and Albert's signature "dee-dah" lick) from the sixth- and ninth-position *B♭* pentatonic minor scales until a high bend to *B♭* signals the return to bopsville. Like Ex. 2 (but without the pull-offs), the IIm–V in bar 3 takes a chromatic approach to a *D♭* Dorian-based run. Here, Stern creates melodic tension by playing a half-step above the IIm chord (*Cm7*). Begin this phrase in the thirteenth position, then shift to twelfth position by playing the *G♭* on beat *two* with your 3rd finger. Shift back to the thirteenth position on the "and" of beat *three* to set up a comfortable fingering for the following Bird-like *B♭* major phrase. Stern subs an *E♭m* Dorian idea over *Cm7* and *F7* before returning inside to *B♭*.

Ex. 3

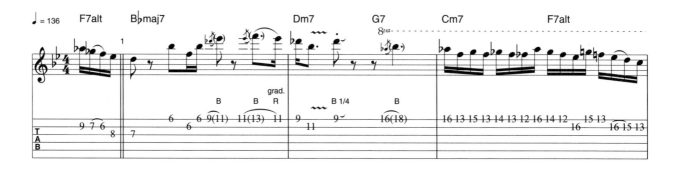

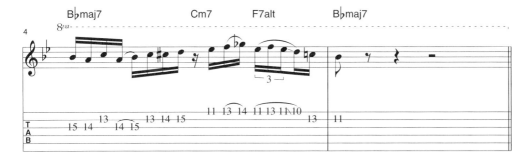

The chromatically descending triad arpeggios in **Ex. 4** are a Stern trademark. He begins inside the *Bb* tonality but quickly heads out to *A*, *Ab*, *G*, and *Gb*, with identical fingerings for each arpeggio. Midway through bar 3 he alters this shape by raising the lower three notes a half-step for a *Gadd#4* arpeggio, reversing the melodic direction and creating additional tension. The line resolves with four ascending diatonic arpeggios.

Ex. 4

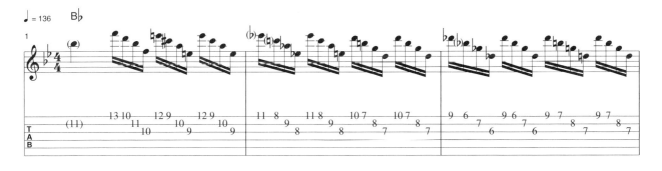

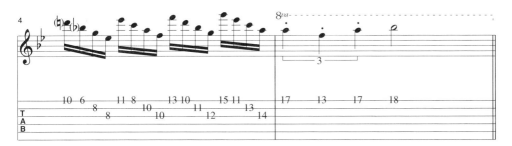

Example 5 is a 16-bar chord-melody chorus. In the two-bar pickup, Mike doubles up the underlying chord changes (*F#m7–B7–Fm7–Bb7* in place of the original *Fm7–Bb7*). Stern then assumes a minimalist single-note stance before introducing two- and three-note voicings over a series of descending IIm–V's. Arriving at *Fm7*, he ascends to the V chord with alternating *Ab* and *Bb* major triads. Once there, he fleshes out the chords with a fourth voice and resolves to *Eb*, using quartal *6/9* chords. In bar 10, Mike sets up a triplet-based rhythmic motif that extends over the IIm–V (*Dm7–G7*) into *C*, with three-note voicings moving beneath a *C* pedal tone. A *C6/9* voiced in 4ths and 5ths precedes syncopated diminished chord punctuations. As a pair of IIm–V's (*Gm7–C7* and *Fm7–Bb7*)

leads us to expect the tonic *Eb*, Stern substitutes a lush, open-voiced *E6/9* that spans more than three octaves with lovely results.

Ex. 5

* or E13

Say What?!

A Lesson with Vernon Reid

Originally published in Guitar Player, *March 1993.*

The letters "WTFF" are Living Colour guitarist Vernon Reid's musical credo. Has he discovered the radio station of his dreams, with ultra-hip DJs on 24-hour call for the most obscure request? No, WTFF is Reid's way of summarizing a concept that defies description, an intangible emotive quality that captures listeners' ears, arouses their curiosity, and makes them crave more. The WTFF can occur in any style of music, and it's even the title of one of the more open-ended tunes on Living Colour's *Stain*. It's an acronym for what Vernon calls the "What The Fuck Factor."

Reid and I discussed this elusive quality in a recent conversation. "Always look for the WTFF," he insists. "If you put on a record and there's none, well, you know what *that* record's worth. On a WTFF scale of 1 to 10, you want to get in there around 7 or 8. If you had 10 all the time, people would just go, 'Huh?'"

Maybe the WTFF springs from a magic combination of innovation, intuition, and passion. "I'm always attracted to 'feel' sorts of things," muses Reid, "but when I hear a player who's really accomplished technically *and* who moves me emotionally, that's the greatest: Pat Martino, Allan Holdsworth, George Benson. Or Joe Diorio—his book *Intervallic Designs* changed my life. They're all very angular, mathematically precise players, but there's something there for me that's very warm. I don't know what it is exactly; maybe a real sense of moral commitment and love. After all, love has angles." Whatever it is, it must be contagious, because the same qualities permeate Vernon's playing, as the following examples demonstrate.

Reid often combines the old and the new. For example, the rockabilly-style turnaround in the second measure of **Ex. 1** sounds fresh because of its unusual harmonic setup in the previous bar. Says Vernon, "It's cool to throw in a little sprinkle of the blues where you might not expect it."

FREE Audio Version **Online**
www.GuitaRev.TrueFire.com

Ex. 1

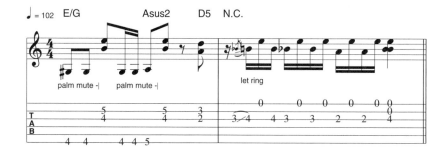

Rhythmic displacement is central to many of Reid's riffs. **Example 2** repeats a three-beat riff over two bars in 4/4. The descending chromatic line at the end of the second measure fills out the remaining two beats so the riff can cycle around again.

Ex. 2

Living Colour sometimes stretches the musical fabric of time; listen, for example, to the incredible ensemble speeding up and slowing down on *Stain*'s "Mind Your Own Business." "If we had approached that academically, we'd have been sweatin' it for a week," Reid laughs. "It was a challenge, but in the end it was fairly easy to do because we all understood it conceptually." The punky riff in **Ex. 3a** is played straight, while **Ex. 3b** warps time via ensemble telepathy.

Ex. 3a

Ex. 3b

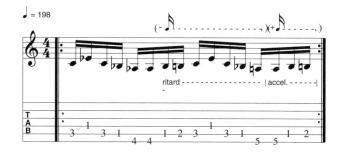

Many of the phrases that fall within what Reid calls his "tritonal thing" wouldn't sound out of place in a Thelonious Monk tune. Consider **Ex. 4**:

Ex. 4

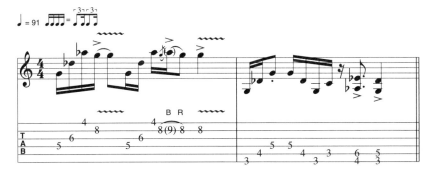

Example 5's four circled "target tones" (notes approached roundabout via adjacent chromatic pitches) form a *Gsus4* arpeggio. Doubled by the bass, this angular riff packs a wallop.

Ex. 5

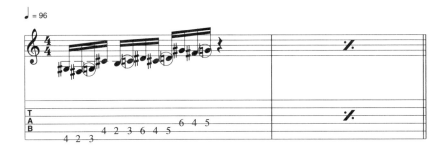

The Monk-meets-Mancini riff in **Ex. 6** features two independent chromatic lines moving in opposite directions on the *E* and *D* strings. "It's one of those film noir, gangsters-on-the-march things," says Reid.

Ex. 6

"I was really happy with my two-handed tapping on this record (*Stain*)," says Reid. The tapped figure that follows the ensemble riff opening **Ex. 7** creates a cascading, bitonal effect. While holding a fifth-position *D(♭5)* chord, Vernon taps out quartal chords (constructed from 4th intervals) that descend in whole-tones. Though all the notes are rhythmically equal, the taps are phrased first as three groups of five and then as four groups of four.

EX. 7

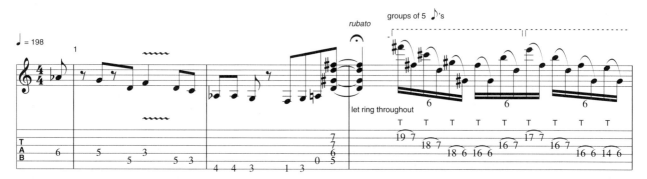

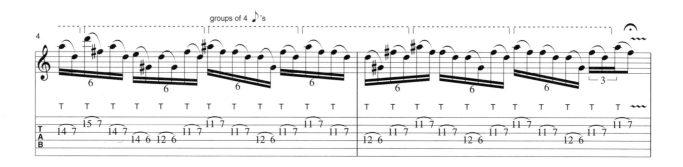

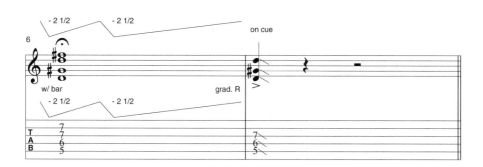

In **Ex. 8**, Reid creates more polytonal tension by playing *E* pentatonic minor lines over an *F* bass figure. The concluding *F* arpeggio sweep locks in with the bass. "It's a little bit of harmonic sleight-of-hand."

Ex. 8

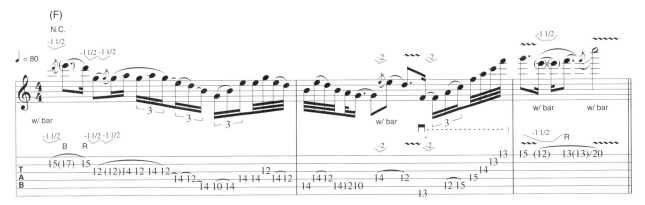

The boppy B♭ major scale motive in **Ex. 9**, from *Stain's* "Ignorance Is Bliss," quotes "If I Only Had a Brain" before proceeding into a Hendrix-y eighth-position *C* pentatonic minor excursion. Reid uses a hard-to-find Electro-Harmonix 16-Second Delay to jump octaves in the middle of the restated *Wizard of Oz* motive, but you can get the same effect with a DigiTech Whammy Pedal or any pitch shifter with a real-time controller. [*Ed. Note: The Electro-Harmonix 16-Second Delay was reissued in 2004.*]

Ex. 9

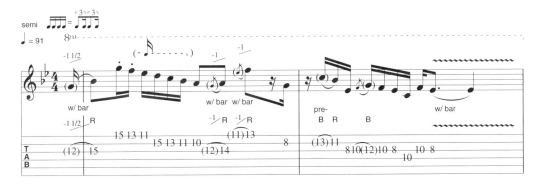

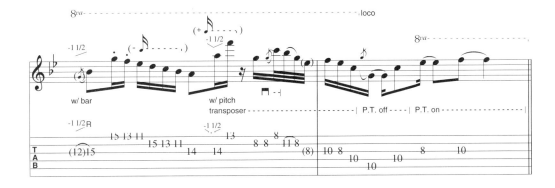

Torn Curtain

Behind David Torn's Psychoactive Sheets of Sound

Originally published in Guitar Player, *September 1996.*

David Torn's musical philosophy reflects the same fierce individualism that earned him the Best Experimental Guitarist title in *GP*'s 25th Annual Readers Poll. "A musician should pursue developing something unique and personal," he stresses. "You can always tell the players who are playing *at* the instrument rather than *playing* it. It's super-critical to develop your own approach. It doesn't matter a fuck if your thing involves releasing anger or has some of the darkness of what people consider to be dissonance. Just find a convincing way to do it. It doesn't have to fit into accepted musical standards. Music is about expression."

But Torn sees a role for discipline in that expression: "It's important to study music and learn what you like in what other people do." In Torn's case, those models include guitarists Jimi Hendrix, John McLaughlin, Wes Montgomery, Mike Bloomfield, Steve Tibbetts, John Abercrombie, and Pat Martino; saxophonists John Coltrane, Dave Liebman, and Jan Garbarek; and the music of northern India and Nepal.

We're at the LooP PooL, the modest but mighty studio in the backyard of Torn's pastoral upstate New York home where he recorded his last two solo albums, *What Means Solid, Traveller?* and *Over God*, and a bevy of scoring projects. Although it's early, Torn is raring to go. "I almost always have a loop going," he says as he straps on his Klein solidbody. He grabs the cheapo salt-shaker mike he keeps in his guitar signal path and waves it in front of his rig to capture a few squeedles of random feedback, then layers single-note volume pedal swells and two sparse E-Bow lines across the thickening texture. A few tweaks of his trusty modified Lexicon PCM-42

mutate his creation into an indescribable sound cluster somewhere between NASA's Voyager recording and the *Forbidden Planet* soundtrack. *Voila!* An ambient loop is born.

Beaming like a proud papa, Torn explains: "I collect these loops on DAT. I must have 30 or 40 DATs full of loops. One of the reasons I like improvising with loops is because there's this random element that you can never repeat exactly because it's *played*—it's not like synthesizers and MIDI." He then adds to the loop soup the minimalistic lines in **Ex. 1a** through **1d**. Studied in isolation, they reveal much about David's signature whammy ornamentation.

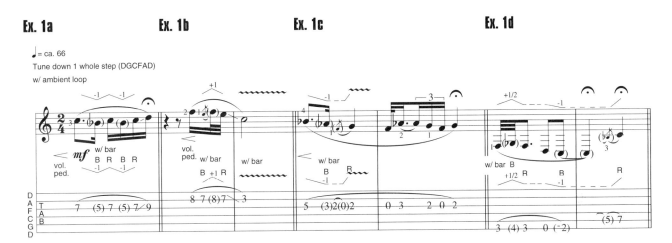

Next, Torn layers an off-the-cuff five-part rhythmic loop with his Lexicon Jam Man (**Ex. 2**). On that device the first punch-in and punch-out establish the loop's tempo, duration, and loop point. David starts with a gritty *G* Phrygian/blues riff that emphasizes the ♭9. The second time around he punches mid-loop and syncopates *G* Phrygian descending from the 5th, then again with offbeat 4ths and a lone 3rd. Note how both phrases cross over the original loop point. Then it's back to the top for the fourth punch, which includes some volume-swelled bass support, followed finally by melodic whammy manipulations of a single harmonic. The combination of rhythmic and ambient loops creates an animated soundscape of stunning complexity and beauty.

"The basis of the writing on *Traveller* was loops of guitar riffs, rhythms, or chord changes. I improvised in free time because I like that feeling of writing that comes from spontaneous, inspired stuff. Then I transfer the loops from DAT to a Logic Audio digital audio sequencer, figure out the tempos, and start constructing pieces around the loops, mixing and matching from within the computer or onto multitrack tape, sometimes just improvising stuff over the top. I'll take sampled rhythms and make them fit the guitar riffs. It's a seriously polarized way of working: On one hand I'm improvising like crazy, and on the other I'm taking the time to arrange these little improvised bits. It can get really twisted."

By now you've probably noticed Torn's penchant for ornamental slurs, slides, and bar bends. "I'll pick a shape of line [such as **Ex. 3a**], but after that, ornamentation is everything for me. I often use the bar [as shown in **Ex. 3b**]." The pitches of Torn's exotic whammy-generated scales are astonishingly accurate. "It's a feel thing," he shrugs. "I use a TransTrem because it's consistent from string to string."

Example 3c, a theme heard throughout "Snail Hair Dune" [from *Polytown*, Torn's '94 collaboration with bassist Mick Karn and drummer Terry Bozzio] utilizes rapidly raised bar slurs for a trilling effect. "The riff is very Arabic-sounding. I transpose it later in the tune."

Ex. 3a   Ex. 3b

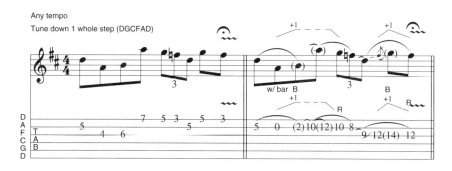

Ex. 3c

* All pitches sound 1/2 step lower than written.

David's finger bends interact so subtly with his bar bends that they're hard to differentiate by ear. He details the tuning and fingering for the wailing main theme of "spell breaks with the weather," *Traveller*'s opening cut (**Ex. 4**). "Some of the bends are slightly flat, some are in-between. I improvised the melody."

Ex. 4

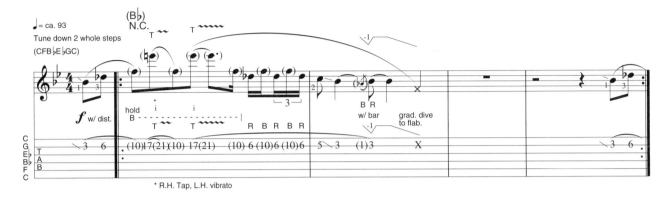

Torn is often bummed by standard tuning. "When I'm playing and recording by myself, I'm super-unhappy if the guitar is tuned to *E*. It feels so damn *small*. I almost always tune down at least to *E♭* and sometimes as low as *B*." He also has a taste for altered tunings. "I love this one," he says as he plays **Ex. 5**'s *DADGCD* figure. "It's like *DADGAD*, except you have a ♭7 on the second string instead of a 5th." This excerpt from *Polytown*'s "Open Letter to the Heart of Diaphora" contrasts David's snaky arpeggio with a quasi-Moorish melody brimming with trademark Torn phrasing. "Because I can pull the bar up a minor 3rd or more, I can get ornaments like you hear in Turkish music." For the recording Torn tuned all the way down to *B*.

Ex. 5

Torn's maniacal soloing on *Traveller*'s ". . . til you are free" (actually the second half of "i will not be free. . .") is a journey in *DADGCD* (transposed a whole-step down to *C*) over an impossibly slow drum groove. "The track was built around a 16-bar drum phrase, sampled and slowed down, though I kept the pitch pretty much the same. Before I improvised the solo, I came up with this lick that I knew I wanted to get to [**Ex. 6**]."

Ex. 6

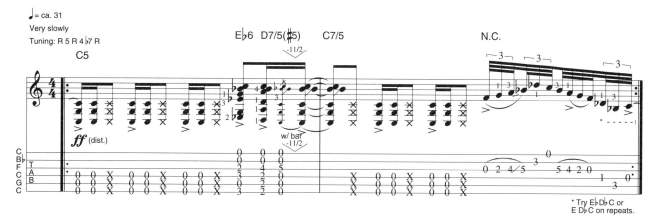

Altered tunings may saddle some players with clichéd stylistic trappings, but not Torn. Examples 7 and 8, from *Traveller*'s title track, were conceived in a lowered version of open *G*, traditionally a country-blues tuning. The exotic riff in **Ex. 7** is well served by the open strings. "This tuning has a lot of lovely things in it," enthuses David. "I put the same tuning on a little mini-Strat and doubled the part an octave higher." Notated in 7/4, 4/4 and 6/4, the figure spans the same time as four bars of 6/4, the tune's primary meter. **Example 8** uses the same tuning for a funky auto-wah excursion driven entirely by ambiguous-sounding parallel minor 3rds (fingered like standard-tuning 4ths) and squawky, Jimi-flavored octaves.

Ex. 7

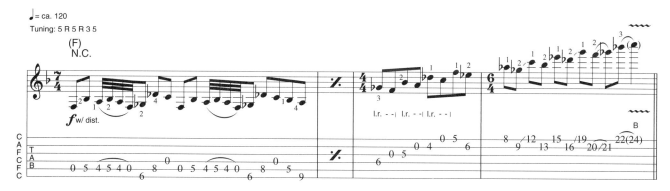

Ex. 8

Given his diverse musings in dropped open *G*, it seems only natural that Torn should coax a sparse, emotionally charged seven-bar blues that oozes Delta authenticity (**Ex. 9**). The tune "... i will not be free" was recorded entirely on one mic with a Framus guitar, Torn recalls. "I went up to Bearsville Studio to visit my friend who produces Cassandra Wilson's records to listen to some mixes, and it was so acoustic and rough and stunningly beautiful that I came back here at 3 a.m. and said, 'Fuck it! I'm putting up a mic, and I'm going to write this tune right now!' I thought I was making a demo. I listened back and thought, 'Damn, I like it the way it is!'" The dramatic chords in bars 4 and 6 of Ex. 9 are harmonically surprising without sounding intrusive.

Ex. 8

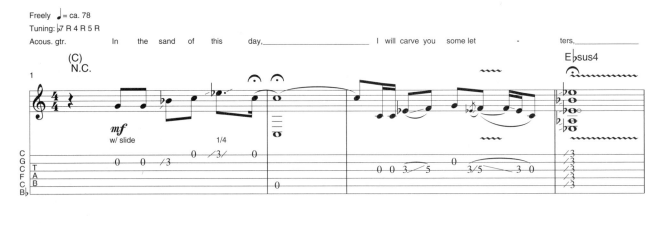

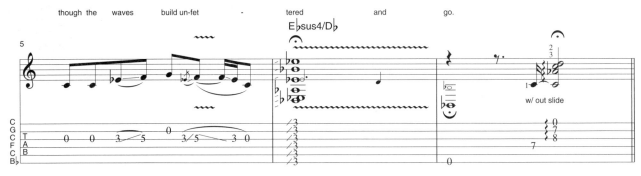

Two CD-ROMs of David's samples, *Tonal Textures* and *Pandora's Box*, have been issued by Q Up Arts (www.quparts.com). The latter contains 70 loops with tempo, pitch, and meter documentation. They are popular with producers, remixers, and sampling keyboardists. Why not try dropping some into your next home movie?

Style Lesson

Consulting the Oracle

A Session with Acoustic Visionary Michael Hedges

Originally published in Guitar Player, March 1997. Michael Hedges was killed in a car crash on December 1, 1997, at age 43.

Michael Hedges' musical tent is miles wide. His influences stretch from the Beatles to Rundgren, Kottke to Mitchell, Crimson to Zappa, Mancini to Martino, Bartók to Schoenberg. How did he craft such a singular guitar style from such diverse influences?

"You listen to people, it goes into your spirit, and then your spirit grows," suggests Hedges between bites of bagel the morning after two devastating sets at New York City's Bottom Line. He uses a recently recorded duet with one of his idols, Pat Martino, to illustrate his point: "If you put me with an electric guitar in standard tuning and tell me to try to play a solo with a jazz band, I'll try to think of something of Pat's that I used to listen to. It's a spiritually charged part of me that emotes Pat. But I don't do much of that — it's more just listening to music and trying to cultivate that musicianship, rather than hands-on guitar work. I don't want to just play the guitar. I want to have ideas and live and enjoy music."

Those sentiments may frustrate those who wish Hedges would focus more on the revolutionary solo acoustic style of his early-'80s recordings. But paradoxically, it's Hedges' refusal to be solely a guitarist that elevates his solo acoustic work above mere fingerboard flash. His Windham Hill album *Oracle* highlights his compositional craft, stylistic breadth, and stunning solo style.

What inspired Hedges to venture beyond the acoustic guitar's conventional picking styles and tunings? "The first catalyst was Leo Kottke's first record (1969's *6- and 12-String Guitar*). That got me into alternating bass lines. I still remember the first thing I wrote just after hearing Leo Kottke." The standard-tuned excerpt shown in **Ex. 1** reveals much about Hedges' formative take on Kottke/Travis fingerpicking, in which the thumb thumps out a rhythmically anchoring quarter-note

FREE Audio Version **Online**

www.GuitaRev.TrueFire.com

bass line while the index and middle fingers play the melody. Bars 14 are based on open-position chords. Pull-offs are introduced in the following *F* and *F#* chords, and the *E/G#* ascends to the fifth position for the next *A* minor section. The progression eventually cycles to the relative major key of *G*. Although the music is notated "let vibrate," Hedges pays meticulous attention to string damping to avoid over-ringing.

Ex. 1

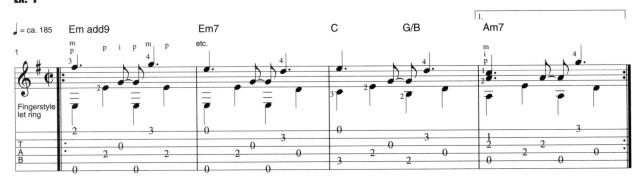

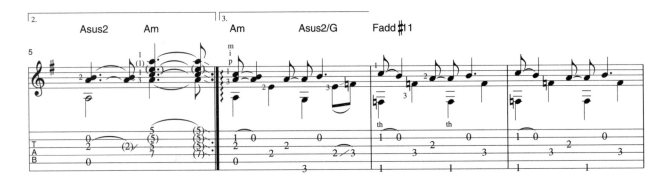

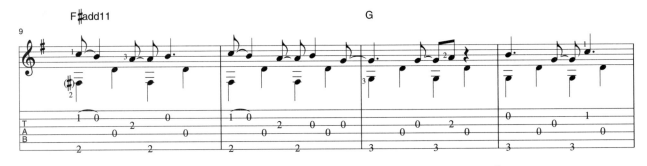

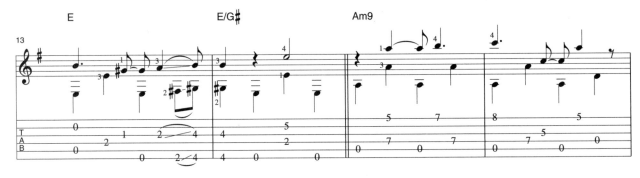

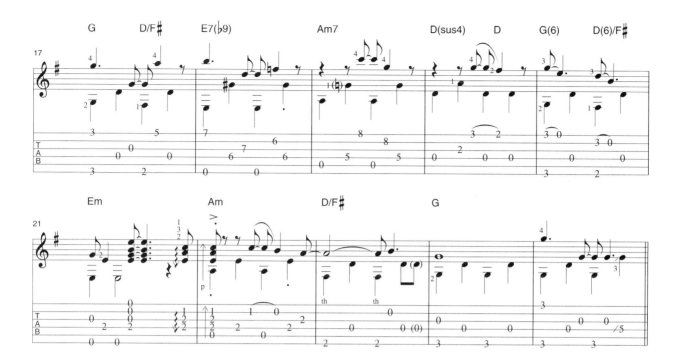

"The second piece I wrote was a little bit more spacey," continues Michael. "I started listening to a lot of Todd Rundgren, and I was trying to get those suspensions." The progression in **Ex. 2** *does* smell particularly Runty, a point Michael drives home by pausing on the *A/G* chord and belting out "city in my head . . ." the opening line from Rundgren's "Utopia Theme."

Ex. 2

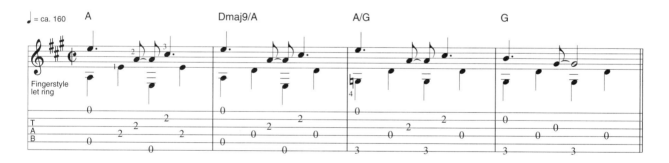

"The next catalyst," he notes, "was Joni Mitchell — a whole different ball game, because she just went wacko with her tunings. She played a lot of open sounds with harmonics, as did David Crosby. The sonorities were all right there; I didn't have to contort to finger them. That's what got me into that style of playing. I was also inspired by something Leo came up with on his first record." Hedges demonstrates with **Ex. 3a**, strumming harmonics and then hammering down left-hand chord shapes while some of the harmonics continue to ring, creating rich polychords like *Em(add4)* over *G*, *Em(add4)* over *D/F#*, and *Bm(add4)* over *C/G*. "That made an indelible mark on my brain. So I tuned my *B* string up to *C* and low *E* down to *D* and wrote 'Silent Anticipation,' the first guitar solo I could call mine."

Ex. 3a

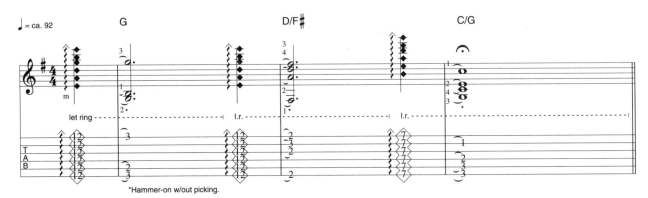

*Hammer-on w/out picking.

Example 3b shows some of the ways Hedges expanded on the technique. After sounding the opening 12th-fret harmonics, bring your fretting hand over the top of the neck and hammer on the bottom three strings at the 10th fret, maintaining enough pressure to sustain the chord. You can lock your middle finger on top of your index for extra whomp. Next, pull off the left-hand barre at the 10th fret while simultaneously stopping the lower three strings at the 12th fret with your right-hand index finger to sound a *D* chord in harmonics over the still-ringing *C* chord. (Yes, natural harmonics are available free of charge on either side of the finger that frets the node!) Then play the three-note *G* chord on the upper strings with conventional 7th-fret harmonics and add another overhand hammer, this time at the 5th fret. Slide the low chord up the neck and then pull off. Finally, play a high *C* chord with 5th-fret harmonics and add an overhand hammer at the 3rd fret for a heavenly *C*-over-*F* sonority. "It's that 'Todd chord' that separates the guitar into two parts," sighs Hedges. "Very simple, but effective."

Ex. 3b

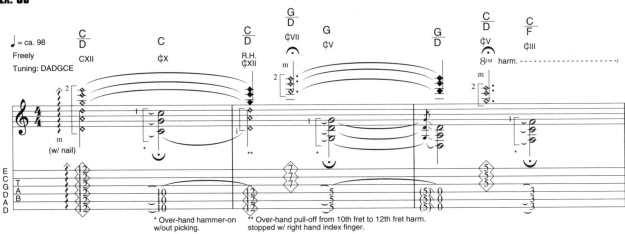

* Over-hand hammer-on w/out picking.

** Over-hand pull-off from 10th fret to 12th fret harm. stopped w/ right hand index finger.

Later Hedges compositions venture into realms entirely his own. The veil-like intro to "Rick-over's Dream" further exploits harmonics generated behind the node. "It's improvised, but it has a form," explains Michael. "I start out with a very light single-note texture, then do the same thing in double-stops. I gradually open it up and add the open *G* and *C* strings. The tuning has a *G* chord on the middle four strings with a *C* on top and a *C* on the bottom." To get a handle on the techniques, begin with the left-hand hammer/pull-off figure in **Ex. 4a**. When that's comfy, elongate the phrase by adding notes on the third string, as shown in **Ex. 4b**.

Ex. 4a   Ex. 4b

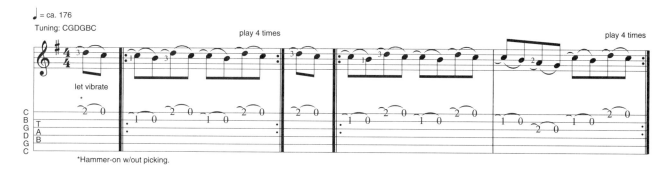

Next, add the harmonics, placing your right-hand index finger over the 12th fret. Use **Ex. 5a** to warm up, and then play the full-length version in **Ex. 5b**. Note that only the pulled-off notes trigger harmonics—the hammered notes (in parentheses) are ghosted or clicked percussively.

Ex. 5a   Ex. 5b

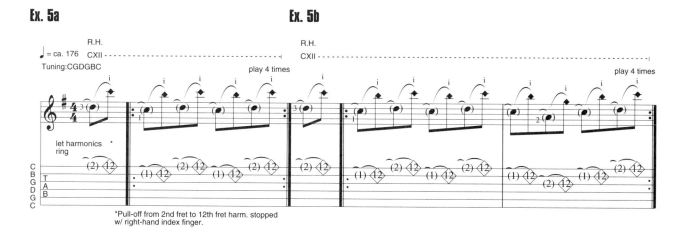

Example 6a introduces double-stops, and **Ex. 6b** deploys them in a longer phrase. Add the 12th-fret right-hand index finger barre for **Ex. 7a** and **7b**.

Ex. 6a   ### Ex. 6b

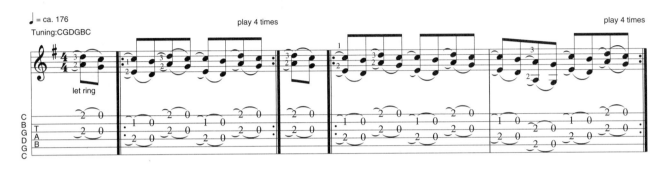

Ex. 7a   ### Ex. 7b

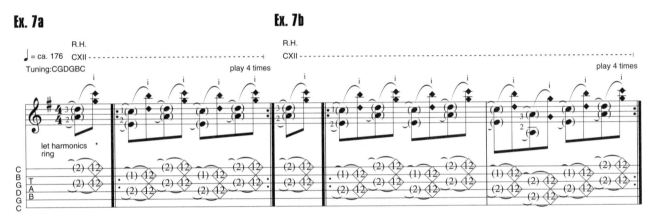

In **Ex. 8**, Michael plays the first half of the phrase in single-note harmonics, then opens up the right-hand barre one string at a time for a mixture of harmonics and open strings—great for that celestial-harp effect.

Ex. 8

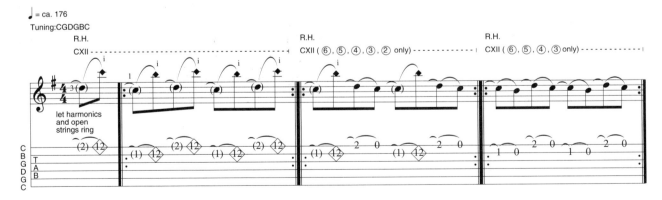

Finally, in **Ex. 9**, Michael applies the same concept using double-stops while gradually opening up the top four strings. In context – over an open *G* or *C* bass – the results are startling as the melodic emphasis shifts between harmonics and open strings.

Ex. 9

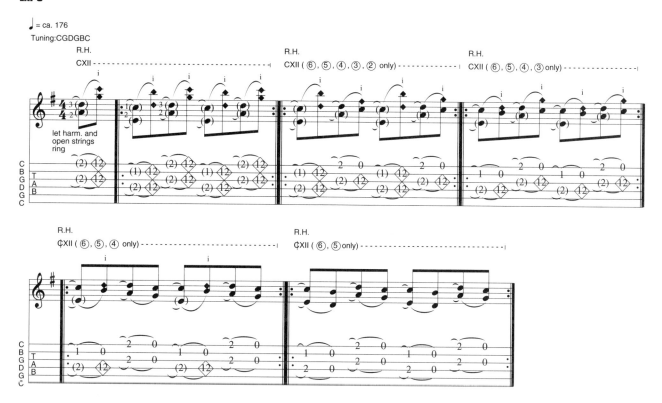

Example 10 explores the sort of arpeggio technique Hedges uses on the intro to "The Second Law," the opening solo from *Oracle*. Michael counters three simple arpeggiated chords with a cascade of open and fretted notes in *AADGBD* tuning. "I feel like I should have orchestrated this," he confides, "but my manager was barking at me to do some solo guitar. It starts with *Am7–G–F*, and then in the last bar the notes all ring out like a harp."

Ex. 10

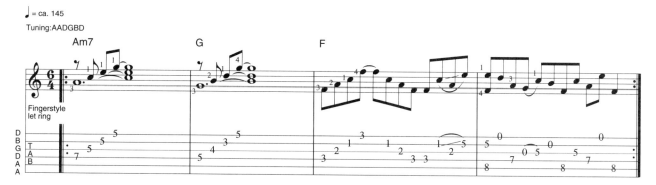

Example 11 demonstrates how Hedges updates the alternating-bass texture of Ex. 1 to accompany vocals on tunes like "Ready or Not." "I like that lick a lot," says Michael. "It's a very strange tuning: *CGDGGG*." Bars 1 and 2, identical except for beat *two*, feature a hammered/tapped *D* note on beat *four*. "When you play the last *G* in bars 1 and 2, it's on a different string, and you get those two different tones. That's why the lick is cool!" The second half of the lick unfolds in another harp-like cascade of a dozen descending scale tones.

Ex. 11

Hedges seems to be wielding a flatpick on more and more tunes. "Jitterboogie," in *DADGAC* tuning, is one of his favorites. "The intro [**Ex. 12a**] is easy," he says. "It's three different *A*'s: an upstroke on the open fifth string, an octave hammer on the sixth and fourth strings at the 7th fret, and then a strum down across all three. The harmonics are on the second, third, and fourth strings; the fifth, fourth and third strings; and then the bottom three strings. You can't always get it exactly, but the idea is to have a little melody on top. It stays on the V chord through the whole intro to get the tension going."

Ex. 12a

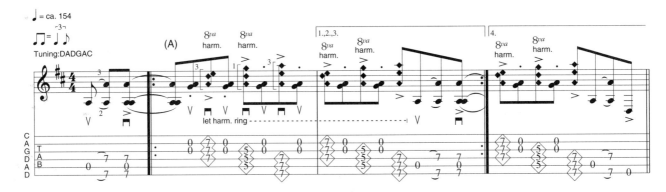

The tonic *D* boogie figure in **Ex. 12b** kicks in with root/5th stabs, muted scratches, and a reverse rake into the classic ♭III–IV crawl, which Michael personalizes with voicings in contrary motion. In the next two bars he intersperses harmonic chimes and some slap-tappin' rhythmic trickery. Starting on *B♭* on the "and" of beat *four*, tap, pick, scratch twice, tap, then pick the harmonics. Michael suggests an onomatopoeic aid: "Think *'ah-chick-ah-de-boom-bah,'* and then get back down however you went."

Ex. 12b

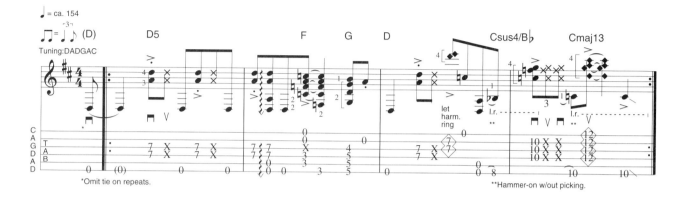

Example 12c presents a tough-sounding variation with a cool chromatic descent over a *D* pedal.

Ex. 12c

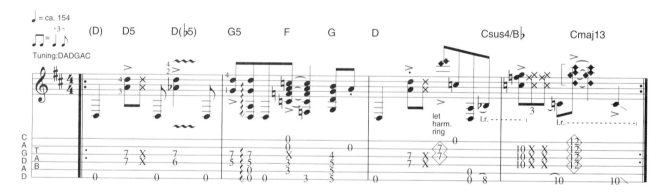

Example 12d is an eight-bar modulation to the key of *G*. "You mute the fifth string with your little finger and then mute the first string with your 1st finger," Michael explains. "In bar 2, mute the first string with the right-hand little finger as you hit the *G/D* chord on the 'and' of *two*." If you rest your pinky on the first string for a beat, you'll be prepped to sound the harmonic on the "and" of *three*. A hammered triplet on the sixth string recycles the figure into fat *D5* and *G5* voicings before returning to the boogie groove.

Ex. 12d

*Pluck harm. w/ R.H. pinky.

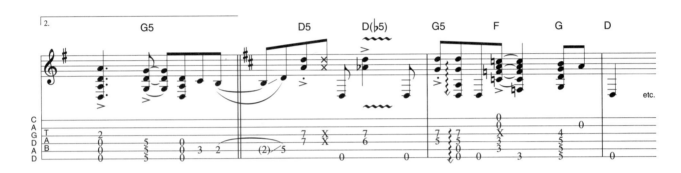

Hungry for more? Hedgehogs who want all the harmonic slaps and knuckle raps should obtain the mind-blowing tome *Michael Hedges: Rhythm, Sonority, Silence* [Stropes Editions]. Co-written by Hedges and John Stropes, this beautifully designed labor of love unlocks the secrets of Hedges' fingerstyle universe. Included are full scores for "Aerial Boundaries," "The Naked Stalk," "Rickover's Dream," and three other compositions, plus a Hedges musical autobiography, essays on composition, electronics, and tunings, a list of all of Hedges' recorded tunings, and other goodies. Stropes' state-of-the-art transcriptions are unquestionably the most accurate and comprehensible Hedges scores available. Stropes Editions, Ltd., 1132 Lake Ave., Racine, WI 53403; 800-733-2520; www.stropes.com.

Recommended Listening

Les Paul
The Legend and the Legacy, Capitol; *20th Century Masters—The Millennium Collection: The Best of Les Paul*, MCA

Jeff Beck
(All on Sony) *Crazy Legs; Frankie's House; Truth; Beck-ola; Beckology; Guitar Shop; Who Else!; Jeff*

Jimi Hendrix
(All on Experience Hendrix) *Electric Ladyland; Are You Experienced; Axis: Bold as Love*

Johnny Winter with Muddy Waters
(All on Sony) *Hard Again; I'm Ready; King Bee*

Duane Allman
(All on Mercury/Universal) *The Allman Brothers Band; Idlewild South; The Allman Brothers Band at Fillmore East*

Carlos Santana
(All on Sony except as noted) *Santana; Abraxas; Caravanserai; Lotus* [Live]; *Supernatural*, BMG/Arista

Stevie Ray Vaughan
(All on Sony) *Texas Flood; Couldn't Stand the Weather; Soul to Soul; In Step*

Allan Holdsworth
I.O.U., Restless; *Metal Fatigue*, Restless; *Road Games*, Globe Music Media; *Against the Clock: The Best of Allan Holdsworth*, Alternity; *All Night Wrong* [Live], Favored Nations

John McLaughlin with the Mahavishnu Orchestra
(All on Sony) *Birds of Fire; The Inner Mounting Flame; Between Nothingness and Eternity; The Lost Trident Sessions*

Steve Vai
(All on Sony except as noted) *Flex-Able; Passion and Warfare; Alive in an Ultra World; Real Illusions: Reflections*, Red Int/Red Ink; *The Infinite Steve Vai*

Joe Satriani
(All on Sony) *Crystal Planet; Surfing with the Alien; Flying in a Blue Dream; The Extremist; The Electric Joe Satriani: An Anthology*

Danny Gatton
Cruisin' Deuces, Elektra; *Redneck Jazz*, NRG; *Unfinished Business*, Powerhouse; *88 Elmira St.*, Elektra; *Untouchable*, NRG; *Hot Rod Guitar: The Danny Gatton Anthology*, Rhino

Mike Stern
(All on Atlantic excepted as noted) *Upside Downside; Play; Standards (and Other Songs); Give and Take; These Times*, ESC

Vernon Reid with Living Colour
(All on Sony) *Stain; Vivid; Time's Up*

David Torn
What Means Solid, Traveller? CMP; *Cloud About Mercury*, ECM; *Tripping Over God*, CMP; *The David Torn Collection*, Times Square

Michael Hedges
(All on Windham Hill) *Oracle; Taproot; Breakfast in the Field; Aerial Boundaries; Live on the Double Planet* [Live]; *Beyond Boundaries: Guitar Solos*

Acknowledgments

I'd like to extend a round of thanks to Richard Johnston, Amy Miller, Matt Kelsey, Kevin Becketti, and Nina Lesowitz at Backbeat Books, and to the past and present editorial staff at *Guitar Player*, especially Tom Wheeler, Jas Obrecht, Lonni Gause, Joe Gore, and Liz Ledgerwood.

As always, my deepest love and gratitude goes to Mary Lou, Dee, and my extended Gress, Tresolini, and Arnold families.

Finally, I bow my headstock to the subjects of this book for boldly going where no guitarist has gone before.

Photo Credits

Pages 1, 31: Michael Ochs Archives.com

Page 9: © Richard McCaffrey / Michael Ochs Archives.com

Page 17: © Bruce Fleming / Michael Ochs Archives.com

Pages 24, 53, 60, 109: © Jon Sievert, Michael Ochs Archives.com

Page 39: © Tom Copi / Michael Ochs Archives.com

Page 45: © Charlyn Zlotnick / Michael Ochs Archives.com

Page 65: © Anna Luken / Michael Ochs Archives.com

Page 74: © Alison Braun / Michael Ochs Archives.com

Page 84: © Daniel Root / Retna Ltd.

Page 93: © David Redfern / Redferns / Retna Ltd.

Page 97: © Joe Hughes / Michael Ochs Archives.com

Page 102: © Jonnie Miles / Retna Ltd.